URBAN MISSION

GOD'S CONCERN FOR THE **CITY**

edited by
John E. Kyle

INTERVARSITY PRESS
DOWNERS GROVE, ILLINOIS 60515

InterVarsity Press is the book-publishing division of InterVarsity Christian Fellowship, a student movement active on campus at hundreds of universities, colleges and schools of nursing. For information about local and regional activities, write Public Relations Dept., InterVarsity Christian Fellowship, 6400 Schroeder Rd., P.O. Box 7895, Madison, WI 53707-7895.

Distributed in Canada through InterVarsity Press, 860 Denison St., Unit 3, Markham, Ontario L3R 4H1, Canada.

All Scripture quotations, unless otherwise indicated, are from the Holy Bible, New International Version. Copyright © 1973, 1978, International Bible Society. Used by permission of Zondervan Bible Publishers.

Portions of chapter fifteen, "Evangelism: The Heart of Missions," are copyrighted and will appear in a forthcoming book and video series from Harper & Row. Used by permission.

ISBN 0-8308-1711-5

Printed in the United States of America.

Library of Congress Cataloging in Publication Data
Urban mission.

Papers presented at the 15th Inter-varsity Student
Missions Convention, held Dec. 27-31, 1987 at the
University of Illinois at Urbana-Champaign.
  1. Missions—Congresses.   2. City missions—
Congresses. 3. Evangelistic work—Congresses.
I. Kyle, John E., 1926-   II. Inter-varsity
Student Missions Convention (15th : 1987 : University
of Illinois at Urbana-Champaign)
BV2390.U73 1988   266'.0097132   88-753
ISBN 0-8308-1711-5

16	15	14	13	12	11	10	9	8	7	6	5	4	3	2	1
99	98	97	96	95	94	93	92	91	90	89	88				

Foreword

Ever since World War 2, we have seen a tremendous increase in migration to the cities of the world. God has enabled us to produce more food with fewer people doing the production work. I think history shows us that farmers tend to be prolific in terms of their families. With fewer jobs on the farm to support a big family, these people have had to go elsewhere to find jobs and make a living. As our farms have become more efficient, we need fewer people to work on them. Those people generally end up in the city. This has been especially true in the U.S., but I believe that in almost every Third World country today, people are leaving the farms and moving to the cities.

For many, many years, evangelicals have been sending missionaries to the foreign mission field. Invariably, that has been to rural areas, as opposed to urban areas. As a youngster, I didn't find my missionary heroes in urban areas. Northcote Deck lived in the Solomon Islands and floated from island to island preaching the gospel. Hudson Taylor—my middle name is Hudson because my mother wanted me to be a missionary to China—worked in the rural areas of China. Bill Deans, a Plymouth Brethren missionary who was a former advertising man went and worked in the Congo. He started a beautiful work in Nyankunde, but it was a rural work. The missionaries I knew about went out as God called them, and they were faithful to the calling God gave them, but none of them went to the cities.

I believe God calls us to go today where people need him. Most of these people are in the cities. In the cities we have grinding poverty, a lot of disease, severe overcrowding, millions of people in a homeless condition. Some of the world's worst conditions are in the cities. Cities are where many hurting people live, and they need to hear the healing gospel of Jesus Christ. Whether it's in the U.S. in the slums of Harlem or Bedford-Stuyvesant, New Delhi, Manila, Tokyo or Mexico City, these major cities of the world are becoming increasingly populated and, for the most part, have never heard the gospel of Jesus Christ. These people need to be told. They need to hear, and they cannot hear without a messenger.

Cities of the world are calling missionaries to service for the Lord which can take many forms: social workers, business people, pastors, teachers, doctors, nurses. There are all sorts of people needed. There isn't anyone who in some way, shape or form could not use the talents they have or the business career they have been involved with to be a missionary to an urban area—either at home or abroad.

I spent most of my adult life working in New York City, and I have been involved in many of the good biblical works in that city. Not only was I involved in missions work and Bible study groups, but I served on the Board of Directors of the United Way and was instrumental in getting money from worldly sources into the hands of the needy and suffering.

Don't think that God calls people to serve only in religious capacities. There are many things you can do within government and within voluntary health and welfare agencies that meet the needs of suffering people. Open doors abound in urban areas today. What we're looking for are people who are willing to go and walk through those doors.

Several years ago I had the opportunity to go to China as a guest of the Chinese government. I lectured with nineteen other advertising agency professionals about advertising and how the Chinese could start up ad agencies and ad-related activities. The people we talked to were tremendously interested in what we had to say. They were open, and in quiet moments, my wife and I had the opportunity to share something of God's Word with them.

When I came back home again, I said to myself, "If I were twenty-one and starting over, China would certainly be the country I would go to. They are hungry for our know-how." They may not be too anxious for us to go out and hold street meetings, but they certainly have no objection to our sharing our faith with the people we would be working with.

I believe there is a tremendous area of opportunity for us today in countries that are closed to missionaries. Professional people, business people of one sort or another can go in, hold down full-time jobs and witness to the saving grace of Christ. These people are particularly useful in the cities of the world, where most of their talents can be put to good use. It doesn't matter what God has called you to do now. There is hardly an excuse for you not being concerned for the lost and dying and for the opportunity you have to use the talents God has given you in another place, most likely an urban area.

May God help you to choose to consider the challenge to be his servant and his messenger to the cities of the world in the 1990s.

Thomas Dunkerton
President, InterVarsity Christian Fellowship

Preface

Imagine 18,700 delegates, thousands of them college students, attending a giant world missions convention in the middle of North America for five days during their Christmas vacation! That's what took place December 27-31, 1987, when InterVarsity Christian Fellowship held its fifteenth student missions convention at the University of Illinois at Urbana-Champaign.

These students were intent on learning all they could about world missions in five days. As one person has said, taking in the heavy content of an Urbana Convention is like drinking water from a fire hose!

Lives were changed during those five short days, and thousands of the delegates will eventually end up as career missionaries. There were over one hundred fifty mission-sending agencies present with over one thousand missionaries on hand to counsel and encourage the delegates. Over fifty educational institutions that teach missions courses were on hand to link up with students needing further training in missions.

The first evening Billy Graham brought a penetrating message entitled, "Are You a Follower of Jesus Christ?" which set the stage for the following days. At the conclusion of his message he was given a standing ovation, after which he requested that those willing to accept Christ as their Savior for the first time should stand for prayer, and hundreds stood. What a way to begin a world missions convention!

The major emphasis of Urbana 87 was on the challenge of reaching the rapidly growing urban centers of our world with the gospel of Jesus Christ. Ray Bakke, Floyd McClung and Harvie Conn brought three major messages on urbanization, the new cutting edge of world missions.

Roberta Hestenes spoke clearly and concisely concerning the importance and possibility of knowing God's will for one's life, including an involvement in world missions, while Becky Pippert explained why evangelism must always be at the very heart of world missions. George Verwer, in his characteristic style, challenged the delegates with a message stressing our need to make Jesus Christ the true Lord of our lives each day we live. Helen Roseveare, veteran missionary to Africa, asked how we can strengthen our motivation for involvement in world missions. All of these messages covered the basics of world missions and were warmly received by the delegates.

Tony Campolo brought a challenging message on the urgency of God's call and asked for decisions at the conclusion of his message. In response, thousands of delegates stood to signify their desire to be involved in world missions. We believe that 15,000 people made written decisions and turned them in before leaving Urbana 87. InterVarsity's Missions Department will follow up on these responses during the next twenty-eight months. Surely the angels in heaven were rejoicing that night!

God greatly blessed the ministry of Ajith Fernando, the Youth for Christ leader in Sri Lanka, as each morning he expounded the book of Jonah. Such challenging and thought-provoking expository teaching by a keen Christian world leader will not be forgotten by the delegates. In preparation for these daily expositions students spent time in personal study followed by participation in one of 2,100 small group Bible studies held throughout the campus. Delegates went away with a new appreciation for this book of the Old Testament and of the theme of Urbana 87, "Should I Not Be Concerned?"

I am thankful for the ministry of the staff of the Urbana Today daily newspaper for providing outstanding news coverage of the convention. What would an Urbana Convention be without multimedia productions of InterVarsity's 2100 team? InterVarsity Press sold thousands of books so that delegates could be served well by taking home small libraries of excellent books.

Finally, my thanks to the Urbana Operations Team that carried out all the logistics of the convention and to all of my InterVarsity fellow staff members across North America who were present to fill all kinds of positions to make the convention go.

Thanks to our wonderful Lord for his presence with us at Urbana 87, because it was his convention and he made it a reality! May you be wonderfully blessed as you read these messages from the Urbana 87 convention.

John E. Kyle
Director, Urbana 87

I
Introduction

1
Why
We are
Here

John Kyle

MY CONVERSION AT THE AGE OF TWENTY-EIGHT ON NEW YEAR'S EVE, 1955, CAN
be summed up in the words of Charles Wesley's hymn:
> Long my imprison'd spirit lay
> Fast bound in sin and nature's night
> Thine eye diffused a quick'ning ray,
> I woke, the dungeon flamed with light;
> My chains fell off, my heart was free,
> I rose, went forth, and followed Thee.

And I have never regretted my decision to follow Christ.

I have a question for each one of us this evening. Why are we here?
No doubt we could come up with various reasons. *Well, my girlfriend
persuaded me to come. My boyfriend persuaded me I ought to be
here. My professor encouraged me.*

These are all good reasons, but why are we really here? Why are
we gathered here from colleges and universities across North America and other parts of the world during our Christmas break? What
is the significance of this particular world missions convention spon-

sored by InterVarsity Christian Fellowship?

I'd like for you to take a trip with me. Twenty-seven years ago my family and I went as missionaries to the Philippines. One of my first field trips was with a missionary who had already served there for five years. Lee took me to an isolated community in northern Luzon—a once famous and now forgotten place where General Yamashita of the Imperial Japanese Navy surrendered in 1945 at the end of World War 2. After an eight-hour bus ride and a six-hour hike in the rain, we finally arrived at our destination at two o'clock in the morning. It was a remote, isolated mountain village.

The next morning was a beautiful day—clear and bright and sparkling. Lee went out and began to distribute the Gospel of Luke to the people of this little community. He and his wife had translated the Gospel into the heart language of this particular group of people— a minority among the many language groups of the Philippines. For the first time in history they had the Word of God, the Gospel of Luke, in their own heart language. Not only had this couple translated the Gospel into their native tongue, they had reduced their language to written form and taught the people to read. It was thrilling to see the expression on these people's faces as they read the Gospel of Luke in their own language for the first time.

As the elders of the community sat in a circle, basking in the sunlight, Lee approached them and gave them a copy of the Gospel of Luke. They were older men and could not read, but Lee gave it to them out of respect. They began to chat back and forth to one another, seemingly discussing the meaning of this event. Curious about what they might be saying, I asked Lee, "Will you translate for me what these men are talking about?"

Lee sat and listened for a while and then said, "It goes something like this:

Our father and our great-grandfathers worshiped all the gods and whenever they went on a long journey they would sacrifice a chicken or a pig. When they planted or harvested a crop they would sacrifice an animal and scatter its blood on the fields. For generations we have been doing this, knowing full well that up here on the mountainside are the footprints of a god that came down and walked across these mountains. And yet we have been worshiping these many gods and appeasing them. Now this young couple has come from across the great waters. They have come here with the message that there is only one God and that this one

God sent his son, one Jesus Christ, here to earth to die for our sins—for all the sins of mankind. It was his blood that was shed to cover all the reasons we have been making sacrifices.

And then they repeated this penetrating question over and over again: "Why has it taken so long for this young couple to come to our little village and to share this news with us?"

I would suggest to you that that couple went there because of the great commission. And one reason we are here is because of the great commission—that is the paramount reason that we are here. Jesus Christ gave to his disciples clear instructions, a mandate, to go into all the world. We find it in Matthew 28:18-20, a familiar passage: "Then Jesus came to them and said, 'All authority in heaven and on earth has been given to me. Therefore go and make disciples of all nations, baptizing them in the name of the Father and of the Son and of the Holy Spirit, and teaching them to obey everything that I have commanded you. And surely I am with you always, to the end of the age.' "

Now much the same command or instruction or mandate is given in the other Gospels. The very last words that Jesus Christ said to his disciples before he ascended into heaven are those recorded in Acts 1:8, "But you will receive power when the Holy Spirit comes on you; and you will be my witnesses in Jerusalem, and in all Judea and Samaria, and to the ends of the earth."

More specifically, we are here because there are 3 billion people who are lost without a knowledge of Jesus Christ. That is an awesome figure. They are in isolated rural villages. They are in suburban areas. But most of them live in the large urban centers of the world—in Calcutta, in Manila, in Singapore, in Nairobi, in São Paulo, in Bogota, in Hong Kong.

And I want to ask you, Should not all of these people, whether on a forgotten island, a rural village or a major city, should they not have an opportunity to know who Jesus Christ is? Should they not have the opportunity to hear in their own language the good news of Jesus Christ, his death, his resurrection, his ascension as living Lord? Should they not have that opportunity? Should they not have the opportunity to say either yes to Jesus Christ or to say, "No, I reject him"?

Historically, students have had a foundational part in world evangelization. There are about 18,000 students here tonight. In a few minutes Billy Graham, a world-renowned evangelist, is going to be speaking to us. Back in 1886 a group of students got together with

Dwight Moody, the greatest evangelist of his time, at Northampton, Massachusetts, for a conference that lasted not for five days, but for a month. Two hundred fifty-seven students gathered together and when the Holy Spirit came upon them, 100 of them gave their lives to become missionaries overseas. The great Student Volunteer Movement was born in 1886 and eventually sent out 2,000 students from secular campuses and Bible institutes from all over North America. The original 100 were sent out by 90 lay people who stayed behind. There were the goers and the senders. Yet their target was only loosely defined.

Today we know what the target really is. People like Ralph Winter and other missiologists have determined that there are some 17,000 unreached people groups around the world. They are the target. The cities of this world are made up of a patchwork of people groups, whether they be the Yuppies of Chicago, the Vietnamese community of San Francisco or the Hispanic immigrants of Los Angeles. These are the targets—we know where they are and we know their needs.

The young people in 1886 had no clear idea of what the target was—they just knew that they were to go to continents, to nations and to cities to proclaim the gospel of Jesus Christ. How fortunate we are to know who the unreached people are. That is your privilege in this generation.

Some people have asked, "Is it possible that in the next thirteen years—before the year 2000 arrives—the gospel of Jesus Christ can be preached all over the world for every group to hear. Can the 3 billion people hear that Jesus Christ is alive, that he died for them, that there is a hope for eternity. Is it possible?"

I believe it is. With all the technology of modern communications, with our knowledge of the hidden people groups, and with the focus on the urban centers of the world, we now have the strategy and means to preach the gospel to all peoples by the year 2000.

Today thousands of young people are streaming to the mission fields every summer, going overseas to experience missions first-hand. Some of them are returning overseas for a two-year term, exercising their gifts and seeing what God can do through them. Many of them have returned home and are gearing up to go out as career missionaries.

Another reason why we are here is to learn how we personally might be mobilized to reach the lost. It is not enough for us to understand the need. It is not enough for us to understand that there are 17,000 unreached people groups around the world. It is not enough to understand that there are 3 billion people who are lost. It is not enough. We must be challenged. We must be motivated to act upon what we know. That is the burden on my heart—that the young people of this generation might be mobilized for mission.

You are a new generation of students in the train of the Student Volunteer Movement and the Student Foreign Mission Fellowship that thrust out thousands of missionaries after World War 2 from Wheaton College, Columbia Bible College and many different secular colleges across North America.

I want to say to you that some of you will leave this convention on New Year's Eve convinced that you should go, that you should make an impact for Christ somewhere in the world. Maybe you'll go as a self-supporting missionary. Maybe you'll go with one of the 150 different agencies that are represented here at Urbana this week. But maybe God will be saying to you very clearly, "I am calling you to stay here and help send others overseas." In God's sight there is no difference between those who send and those who go.

I stand before you this evening because there are at least twenty-five churches that support my wife and me that we might have this ministry. It is important that there be senders. It is important that there be goers. The job can't be done without both. I want to challenge you as you're here. I want you to be sensitive to the leadership of the Holy Spirit, sensitive to what God might say to you this week. When you come to this assembly hall, bow your head in prayer and say, "Lord, help me to hear what I need to hear."

Because my missionary friend responded to the great commission thirty-two years ago, today in those mountain villages there are churches. The people have the whole Bible in their own language. They have their own preachers. They have their own hymn book. They have their own missionaries to reach out to others—all because a couple were obedient to God. And many of their friends, fellow students, stood behind them and prayed for them. God bless you as you have the opportunity to be challenged and motivated for world mission this week.

John Kyle, now director of Mission to the World, served as missions director for InterVarsity Christian Fellowship for ten years and as director for the 1979, 1981, 1984 and 1987 Urbana Conventions.

II
Should I Not
Be Concerned?
Exposition
of the
Book of Jonah

2
Running Away from God
Jonah 1:1-16

Ajith Fernando

THE BOOK OF JONAH BEGINS BY SAYING, "THE WORD OF THE LORD CAME TO Jonah son of Amittai." Who is this man Jonah? He lived at the time in the Jewish nation when it was divided into two groups. In the north was Israel, and in the south was the kingdom of Judah. Jonah was from the northern kingdom. He lived about the eighth century before Christ. He is mentioned in 2 Kings 14:25 as a prophet from Gath Hepher, who prophesied that Jeroboam the king of Israel would restore the boundaries of Israel, and it was fulfilled during his own lifetime. So obviously Jonah was a person with some respect in society. Incidentally, Gath Hepher is in Galilee, so when the Pharisees said that no prophet comes from Galilee, they were wrong, because Jonah had come from Galilee.

Jonah's Strange Commission
Verse 1 tells us that "the word of the LORD came to Jonah." This is a common biblical way of saying that God had communicated his message to his prophet. How exactly it was communicated we are

not told. Perhaps it was done in different ways at different times—through dreams, through visions, through a strong impression in the mind of the prophet—and it came to be called the word of the Lord.

Verse 2 tells us that the word of the Lord came to Jonah the son of Amittai and said, "Go to the great city of Nineveh and preach against it, because its wickedness has come up before me." Now this is a very hard commission. No prophet before this had been sent to the streets of another nation to preach judgment. Elijah was sent to the nations but never with a message like this.

Nineveh was quite a distance away, probably over six hundred miles as the crow flies, and about seven hundred-fifty miles by road. And Jonah probably had to walk. It was a very big city with many people. Here was a lone person from another country asked to go and make contacts there and to preach against this city—a very difficult task.

As a Jew, Jonah must have had all sorts of problems about going and preaching to Gentiles. There were theological blocks that prevented him from doing this, and we are told that Nineveh was a wicked city. They were enemies of Israel, and they were very well known for the ways in which they were cruel to their enemies. Jonah was asked to go and preach against this city.

There is a cartoon by Kurt Mitchell in a children's book that expresses Jonah's dilemma very well. In this cartoon Jonah is depicted as a mouse and the people of Nineveh as cats. This mouse is asked to go and preach to the cats. Someone has said it was like asking a Jewish rabbi in 1943 to go to Berlin and cry against the wickedness of the people there—a very hard job.

But the call of God is often like this. It takes us to places which others regard as impossible, to do work which looks like utter folly. Of course, with the call of God comes God's provision, but we don't always see that at the start.

World Evangelism Today
The work of world evangelism looks something like this at the end of the twentieth century. What we think of as sacrificial service, the world regards as arrogant imposition. Christians in Sri Lanka, for example, are embarrassed by our historical connections with the colonial rulers. Non-Christians and even some Christians think that evangelism is an extension of this colonial spirit—the same spirit of arrogance that tries to impose our will on others. It's nothing of the

sort! But that's the way people think about it. Also, the world's religions are experiencing a resurgence now, and they too have developed a missionary zeal. So ours is not an easy call.

Just a few weeks ago we had a very unusual meeting, and the majority of the people at that meeting were Hindus. My colleague who was preaching there presented very clearly the message that Christ is unique and that he is the only savior. A section of the audience was so enraged by what he said that they wanted to assault him. But a few of those who attended heard the message, accepted it and gave their lives to Christ.

Sometimes the temptation comes to us to downplay evangelism, for it implies the need for people to discard their old ways and to follow Jesus Christ as their only savior. But we must not and we cannot downplay evangelism if we are obedient to God.

The call of Jonah was costly, just as our call will be costly. The Lord will teach us to preach against the city because its wickedness has come up before him.

Now this expression, *preaching against the city*, suggests that we are to present God as a judge who has been sinned against. This is a familiar theme in the Scriptures. We preach to people not only because we have good news that God loves people—that is our primary message—but also because people's sins have come up against God, because they are lost and headed for judgment. We must not forget this fact.

Running from God
In verse 3 we are told that Jonah ran away from the Lord and headed for Tarshish. Tarshish is probably Tartessus, a town in Spain. It was a town far west of Palestine, on the western edge of the world they knew about. Nineveh was on the eastern edge of the world they knew about. Jonah was asked to go to the far eastern edge of their world, but he went to the far west.

Now you might ask, "Why didn't Jonah stay in the comfort of his home in Palestine? If he wanted to disobey God, why did he have to go all the way to Tarshish?" Well, Tarshish was a place where you would least expect a revelation from God. The people there didn't know the Lord. Being disobedient to God is extremely uncomfortable, and when you're disobedient to God and meet God's people, you become even more uncomfortable. So Jonah wanted to be a safe distance from anything that reminded him of God.

Isn't that true even today? When people are living in disobedience, they often avoid close contact with Christians. They miss church; they don't come to the small group meeting. Sometimes they give very legitimate reasons as to why they can't come, but the real reason is that they want to avoid the discomfort of being with Christians. If they do come to the meeting, they rush off before anyone catches them for a conversation.

Jonah went to Tarshish, and we are told that he ran away from the Lord. From chapter 2 we know that Jonah was well-versed in the psalms. He would have known that the psalms teach that God is everywhere, that he is omnipresent. How then could he run away from God? In the first place, he could run away from the will of God. He remained a Jew; he did not discard his belief; he did not commit any great sins; but he did not do what God wanted him to do. And to disobey God is to run away from God! Not only that, to run away from the will of God is also to run away from the presence of God. God was there, but Jonah closed the door to experiencing the presence of God in his life.

Psalm 119:165 says, "Great peace have they who love your law." When we obey God, we live with God, and he lives with us. Jesus put it this way in John 15:4: "Remain in me, and I will remain in you." When you do that, you have complete peace. Isaiah 26:3 states that when a person's mind is steadfast—steadfast in faithfulness to God alone—God will keep that person in perfect peace. That is the great privilege of the Christian. It is not an easy life. There's a lot of heartache, but there is also the peace of God's presence.

As John Wesley lay dying, suffering during the last few moments of his life, he kept repeating this statement, "The best of all is God is with us." That's the great joy of being a Christian!

David Livingstone, who went as a pioneer missionary to what was known as the dark continent of Africa, was once asked what kept him going amid all the struggles he faced. And what struggles they were! He was attacked and maimed by a lion. His body was often racked by fever and dysentery. The one home that he built was burned down during the Boer War. His wife died on the field, and most of the time he was all alone. When he was asked what kept him going, he said that the word of Christ kept ringing in his ears, "Lo, I am with you always, even to the end of the world."

David Livingstone also said, "Without Christ not one step, with him anywhere." We are told that once, when he was asked about the sacrifices he made, he became angry and said, "Sacrifice? The only sacrifice is to be outside the will of God!" When you do that, you forfeit the presence of God and the peace that endures. That's what was happening to Jonah.

In the second part of verse we are told that Jonah went to Joppa, and he found a ship bound for the port of Tarshish. After paying the fare, he went on board and sailed for Tarshish to flee from the Lord.

Going Down to Joppa

Why does the author say Jonah went *down* to Joppa? Actually, this is one of the four times this word *down* is mentioned in this passage. It doesn't appear in the New International Version, but in the King James Version the word *down* appears four times. Verse 3 states, he "went down to Joppa." Then he went "down into" the ship. In verse 5 we are told that Jonah had gone "down into the sides of the ship." Then in 2:6 Jonah says, "I went down to the bottoms of the mountains."

This repetition of the word *down* is obviously very significant. The person who wrote Jonah was a literary artist. He used a lot of literary devices, which make Jonah a very beautiful book. To go away from the will of God is to go *down*. It may have looked as if Jonah was not going down. In fact, he would have had to pay a big fare to get into that ship. He was acting like a rich man, a person of status. But because he was going away from God's will, he was going down, even though it did not look that way.

Some people are making a lot of money, enjoying high standards, maybe even giving a lot of money for the work of God. Although they have climbed in society, they have actually gone down rather than up, because in their climb they moved away from God's will. They thought they were climbing up, but they were so disoriented that they didn't realize they were really climbing down.

Most of you are at a crucial stage of your life. You are bounding with enthusiasm to make your life count. There will be times along the way when you will be tempted to compromise. Maybe it will be a choice of a spouse who does not share the vision you have. Perhaps it will be getting caught up in the quest for success which drowns the other voices from your life. Maybe it will be a decision to refuse God's call for you, because that call is too costly. Perhaps you will climb in society, but that will be a climbing down in life. Each step will be a step away from joy or being part of the agenda of the kingdom which will ultimately conquer and rule the world.

It is interesting that many centuries later, Peter made a momentous decision from that same city of Joppa. While he was praying, God told him to go to Caesarea to the home of a Gentile named Cornelius to preach the gospel. To a Jew this was a surprising request. In fact, members of the church questioned him about it. But Peter obeyed implicitly and laid one of the key building blocks in the history of the growth of the church. As he went to the house of Cornelius, he preached the gospel and the first Gentiles were converted to Christ.

As you leave Urbana, which way will you go—to Caesarea or to Tarshish? Will you be like Peter or like Jonah—up on the road of obedience or down on the road of disobedience? Jonah went down.

Jonah's Humiliation

According to verse 4, the Lord sent such a violent storm on the sea that the ship threatened to break up. Jonah had tried to run away from God, but all he succeeded in doing was forfeiting the peace of God's presence. Then suddenly he had to face the power of God's presence! God was there, and he showed himself in great power.

We are told in verse 5 that all the sailors were afraid, and each one cried to his own god. When their prayer didn't seem to work, they were forced to do something a little more costly—they threw out the cargo to lighten the ship, but that, too, didn't work.

In the third part of verse 5 we are told: "But Jonah had gone below deck, where he lay down and fell into a deep sleep." While the Gentiles are desperately seeking a solution—but looking in the wrong place—the servant of the living God, who knows the solution, is fast asleep.

Possibly Jonah was exhausted after running fast to Joppa to get away from the presence of the Lord—but what a sad sight! The people of the world are looking desperately for an answer, and they don't know where to go or what to do, and the one who knows the answer is asleep! What criminal negligence, we would say.

But could that be said of us too? Living in a world of such need, we who have found the One who is the only answer to that need are in the slumber of our disobedience!

The captain went to him and said, "How can you sleep? Get up and call on your god! Maybe he will take notice of us, and we will not perish." What a humiliating awakening for this servant of God, this respected prophet of the Lord. He is not being persecuted for his failure. He is not being ridiculed for his beliefs. He is being justifiably scolded by an unbeliever for being in the wrong place.

The servants of God are humiliated when they are caught in the wrong place because of their own disobedience. For example, a Christian witness is humiliated when a person he has witnessed to sees him coming out of a pornographic book store. A Christian student is humiliated when she is caught cheating on a term paper. A Christian youth is humiliated when he is justifiably rebuked by his non-Christian parents for his own selfishness—a child of the light, justifiably rebuked by a child of darkness, an ambassador of the King of kings and Lord of lords, rebuked by one to whom he is supposed to introduce the King. What a contrast our call from Jesus is: "Let your light shine before men, that they may see your good deeds and praise your Father in heaven" (Mt 5:16).

The captain asked Jonah to pray to his god. He may have thought: the other gods have been tried; this god may have been left out. We don't know how Jonah responded to the captain's request. He may have just murmured something and sheepishly followed the captain to the deck.

The sailors said: "Come, let us cast lots to find out who is responsible for this calamity." They had tried prayer, and it didn't work. Then they tried throwing something away, and that didn't work. They seemed to have been convinced that there was something out of the ordinary in this storm. Perhaps they thought there was somebody responsible for this situation—someone with a curse on him. They said to themselves: "A lot may reveal the guilty person." So they cast lots, and the lot fell upon Jonah. The Lord sovereignly intervened, and Jonah was caught!

In verse 8 the sailors asked Jonah, "Tell us, who is responsible for making all this trouble for us? What do you do? Where do you come from? What is your country? From what people are you?" These sailors were quite honorable people. There was a lot of desperation in their tone, but they didn't manhandle Jonah, they just questioned him.

Jonah answered, "I am a Hebrew and I worship the LORD, the God of heaven, who made the sea and the land." "I am a Hebrew"—that's how the neighbors identified Jews. "I worship the LORD"—in the original Hebrew it was YHWH. There were no vowels in the original Hebrew, and when people added vowels they pronounced YHWH as "Jehovah." This was the specifically Israelite name of the Lord, his personal name. It was not used by others, so Jonah was describing God as the God of Israel.

The God of Heaven

Then Jonah goes on to describe God a little further. He says, "the God of heaven, who made the sea and the land." This word "God" is from the Hebrew word *Elohim*, which was the common word for God in the ancient Near East. It is the word from which we get Allah, the word Muslims use for God. But he's not just any God, he is the "God of heaven." He is not just a local deity; he is the sovereign God. Jonah is trying to tell these people that this is the greatest God that there is. Then he expresses God's supremacy more clearly by stating that he made the sea and the land. He is the creator of everything. So the sailors realize then that nothing can stop this storm. The Creator himself is responsible.

This is the biblical way to introduce God to non-Christians. He is presented as supreme, and he is presented as Creator. This is how Paul, for example, introduced God when he was speaking in Lystra and Athens to the people who were not Christians, who had no biblical background. When we witness to Buddhists and Hindus in Sri Lanka, one of the first things we stress is the fact that God is the Creator. In our evangelistic camps in Youth for Christ the first session that we have is on the creation. That is the basic thing we need to establish.

I have a dear friend in Sri Lanka who was a devout Buddhist. A fellow student on campus told him about Jesus Christ and took him to an InterVarsity meeting. After he went to that meeting, he said that Christianity just didn't make any sense—especially the idea of Jesus Christ dying for the sins of other people. He just couldn't stand it. It seemed like nonsense until he realized that God is Creator. When he realized that, everything else began to fall into place. Last month he was baptized as a Christian.

We see the effectiveness of this in the sailors' reaction in verse 10. We are told that when Jonah said this, it terrified them. The sailors had been frightened by the storm, but their fear becomes terror when they realize that they are dealing with the supreme God.

The evangelistic value of establishing the supremacy of God is very clear here. There are tremendous repercussions when a person becomes a Christian. All sorts of problems come. The new Christian wonders, "Will my relatives go against me? Will all these people persecute me?" And they are afraid. Then we present to them the fact that God is the creator of the universe. He is supreme. He is greater than all the gods and the masters of this world. Therefore, if he is so great, the wisest thing to do is to follow him.

When Jonah told them that, they asked him, "What have you done?" They were saying in effect, "How could you do such a thing?" They were pointing out to Jonah the folly of his disobedience. What follows is a very interesting parenthesis: they knew he was running away from the Lord because he had already told them so. Why then didn't they scold him when he told them at the start?

In everyday life it is the obedient person, the one who pays the price of following God's ways, who looks like a fool. The world looks at the sacrifices we make, and they think we are fools. They feel sorry for us. The way of obedience results in victory, but for a moment it seems as if the way of obedience is a difficult way. God will ultimately reveal the real situation, but until then people see what looks like the folly of obedience.

That's what happened in Jonah's case. When Jonah first told them he was running away from the Lord, it did not strike them as something special. Then came the revelation of God in the storm, and they saw the facts as they were. They realized the folly of disobedience, and when they realized it, they said, "What a fool you are!"

I hope this sobers us. So many people choose the path of folly because they think it's the best way. The way of obedience seems to cost too much. The price seems to be too high. They win acclaim on earth, but when the Lord reveals himself—and he will some day—we realize the folly of following the way of the world. "The world and its desires pass away" says the apostle John, "but the one who does the will of God lives forever" (1 Jn 2:17).

Jonah Faces Up to His Sin

The sea was getting rougher and rougher. So they asked Jonah, "What should we do to you to make the sea calm down for us?" "Pick me up and throw me into the sea," he replied, "and it will become calm. I know that it is my fault that this great storm has come upon you." Jonah's godly character finally shines through. He is willing to die so that others on the ship will be saved. He has run away from God, he has nowhere to go. Now he says, "Lord, take me."

I wonder if this is why Jesus compared Jonah to himself. Jesus gave himself so that the world would live. Jonah gave himself so that the sailors might live. But these sailors prove to be too honorable to let Jonah die like that, so they try to row back to the land. Then the sea grows wilder than before. God was not going to short-circuit the process of Jonah's repentance. Jonah's sin was so serious that he had to face up to the full implication of his sin. There was no shortcut to his repentance. He had to face up to that. And Jonah had to face up to his sin before he received God's full restoration. Remember that.

Let me conclude by saying that the most prominent objection to Christianity I have heard from Buddhists and Hindus is: "Your forgiveness is cheap. You receive God's forgiveness and live any way that you like." The implication is that Christianity is cheap. They think their religion is more noble because they take sin seriously.

My dear friends, the Bible says God does take sin seriously, and we cannot trifle with it. This is the lesson God taught Jonah. It is the central theme of this passage. God is holy. We cannot run away from him. It is folly to try. If you are trying to run away from God, let me tell you that it is useless. All your excuses are too weak to stand the scrutiny of God's holy wisdom. Come back to him. Come back before it's too late. Don't wait for God to do something drastic like sending you to the bottom of the sea.

3
Praise for Deliverance
Jonah 1:17—2:10

Ajith Fernando

NEAR THE END OF CHAPTER ONE WE FIND JONAH IN A DESPERATE STATE, THROWN into the sea with no hope of survival. But the situation begins to change at 1:17 as God intervenes once more. Verse 17 states: "But the Lord provided a great fish to swallow Jonah, and Jonah was inside the fish three days and three nights."

Problems Related to the Big Fish

Pardon the pun, but people have had a whale of a time discussing the various points concerning this fish! So much so that it has detracted from the great message of this book. G. Campbell Morgan has said, "Men have been looking so hard at the great fish that they have failed to see the great God."

Some have gone to great lengths to discover the identity of this fish and to prove that what happened could indeed have happened. Some have tried to show other instances where people and dogs, for example, have stayed inside big fish for considerable lengths of time. Now I don't think any of them were inside a fish for as long as three days, but these instances show us that such things can happen and that the story of Jonah is not as impossible as some people think.

We must remember, however, that the story of Jonah and the fish is presented as a miracle. Miracles supersede the laws of nature. So our belief that this happened does not depend on whether or not it can happen in everyday life under the normal circumstances. We are not told what type of fish this is. For example, we do not know whether it was a whale. The King James Version translates Jesus' word in Matthew 12:40 as "whale," but that is a mistranslation. We don't know exactly what happened, but we do know that Jonah was inside the fish for three days.

Others have used this story to show that Jonah is not a historical book. They have compared this story with similar myths about great fish, and they say that this gives evidence that the book is only a parable. Some say that the fish is a symbol of some monster like Nebuchadnezzar, the Babylonian conqueror of the Jews.

Sinclair Ferguson, in his book *Man Overboard,* observes that this must be the most criticized fish that ever swam in the Mediterranean. But these critics of the story disregard that the Scriptures record miraculous events. The Bible is very clear that God intervenes miraculously, especially during periods of special revelation, periods when the Scriptures are being written and he wants to reveal his will and his ways in an unmistakably clear way.

Even those who accept the miraculous sometimes question whether this could really have happened. Some feel that the story is a parable and did not actually take place. Now I must say that there is a very strong place for parables in Scripture. In fact, there is a clearly parabolic element in the book of Jonah, but that does not mean the book is not historical. Those who wish to explore arguments for the historical reliability of Jonah can look at some of the standard treatments. Let me just recommend one small commentary. It is on Jonah and Nahum by John Kohlenberger. It is nontechnical but quite well done.

The Message Conveyed by the Big Fish

If there is a parabolic element in this book, what could be signified by this great fish? Why did God choose this unusual way to save Jonah? In 1:13 we are told that the mariners tried to row to shore, so they must have been fairly close to shore. Surely, God could have provided a piece of floating wreckage and could have directed that wreckage to the shore.

Possibly God chose this fish because it represented something peo-ple at that time greatly feared, especially the Jews. In ancient mythol-ogy the big fish represented what was known as Leviathan, the sea monster. It is interesting that the word Jesus used when talking of Jonah being in this fish could be translated "sea monster." Leviathan is often mentioned in the Old Testament, especially in the poetic books, as a fearsome creature of the sea. This doesn't mean that people believed the myths about Leviathan, but they used them in much the same way as we when we refer to fairies or the boogieman.

Leviathan represented the powerful monster of the sea. So, for example, Jonah speaks of being in the fish as being in "Sheol," the place of the dead (v. 2). It was as if God was saying that this thing of great power, this thing which signifies death and destruction, even this thing God can use to fulfill his purposes. Even the monster of the sea is at the disposal of God! So the provision of this fish is an example of God's sovereignty. This is a theme which is very important in Jonah and in the whole Bible: God is more powerful than all of the forces of evil in the world, and he can use even the forces of evil to fulfill his purposes.

In the past four and one-half years, we in Sri Lanka have lived amid much turmoil. There has been a lot of death and destruction and violence. During this time, I think no doctrine has seemed more rele-vant to me than the doctrine of God's sovereignty. At a time when evil seems to have a field day, I know that the will of God will finally conquer. And if that is so, the greatest need for us is to align ourselves with the will of God. When we align ourselves with the will of God, we are traveling with the stream that ultimately leads to victory.

About two months ago, I had to take a difficult trip. Three of our staff had been very badly bruised and assaulted, and a colleague of mine and I had to travel to a fairly unsafe place. There were a lot of questions. Should I go? Should someone else go? We have only one vehicle we use for Christ. Should we take this one van? Various things were going through our minds. There was a lot of uncertainty. Then we decided, after praying, that we would go. Until we had decided that, there was a lot of uncertainty in my mind. Once the decision was made, there was a peace. Why? I knew we were traveling along God's will, and when we follow God's will, there is no fear. God would turn this thing to victory by whatever means. Through death or through life, God would use it for his glory.

I have a colleague named Suri Williams who ministers in the most dangerous place in Sri Lanka, a place called Jaffna. We have given him the freedom to come back if he wishes. He has chosen to stay there along with his wife and two children. They have lived through some very, very scary experiences. Suri often tells us the safest place to be is in the center of God's will. Why? Because God is sovereign and, if he finds us open to him, he will work his great purposes through us even in the midst of untold evil. That is what Jonah found out. When he faced up to the full implications of his sin and committed himself to the deep blue sea, to certain death, God acted sovereignly to rescue him using the very thing that people of that time feared so much.

Jonah's Song of Praise

We don't know what happened to Jonah the moment he was thrown out of his boat. Was he swallowed at once in a conscious state? Or had he half-drowned and lost consciousness? Some people even think he died. If he did lose consciousness, which is quite likely, he would have got quite a shock when he awoke. "Is this the bottom of the sea? It's very dark but relatively dry. Is this Sheol, the place of the dead? Something fishy is going on here!" The truth would have finally dawned on him. He was still alive, and while there is life, there is hope. God had acted on his behalf.

Jonah 2:1 states, "From inside the fish Jonah prayed to the LORD [Yahweh] his God." Note the way the relationship with God is described: "Yahweh his God." Jonah is no longer running away from God. He is God's servant, enjoying an intimate relationship with God again, and his joy expresses itself in a prayer.

Jonah's prayer follows a pattern of a certain type of psalm in the Bible that is given in response to God's salvation. The Jews used different types of prayers to help them respond to different situations. These prayers enabled them to make praise and thanksgiving part of their lifestyle. How often we neglect to thank God after a prayer is answered. We pray very hard to God, but when he answers we forget to thank him, because praise has not become part of our lifestyle.

Let me use a Sri Lankan example. One hot, humid day a lady came by bus to visit her sister. The bus dropped her in town, and she had a long walk to her sister's home. She walked in the hot sun with the beads of perspiration running down her. As she walked and entered the house, her nephew came and said, "Auntie, my rubber ball broke yesterday. Would you please give me a new ball?"

The auntie turned, went back outside and walked to the center of the town. After half an hour, she returned with the ball, tired and perspiring. The boy grabbed the ball from his aunt and ran away to play with it. Now we would rebuke that boy for ingratitude. But that's precisely what we often do when we don't stop to say thank you. The Jews had formal prayers to help them thank God. These had become part of their lifestyle.

Let's look at this Jewish song of praise that Jonah prayed. Usually these songs of praise had six parts. The first part was a *proclamation,* something like, "I will praise you." This part is missing in this particular psalm. The second part was what we might call an *introductory summary,* which summarized the occasion for praise. This is what we see in verse 2, which says, "In my distress I called to the LORD, and he answered me." Then there follows a parallel statement. (Jewish poetry, uses parallelism rather than rhyme.) "From the depths of the grave I called for help, and you listened to my cry." Jonah was saying that God had delivered him from certain death.

The third part of the prayer *looks back to the time of need.* Verses 3-6 describe the depths of Jonah's hopelessness. "You hurled me into the deep, into the very heart of the seas, and the currents swirled about me; all your waves and breakers swept over me." Verse 4 continues, "I said, 'I have been banished from your sight; yet I will look again toward your holy temple.' "

A ray of hope there—but just for a moment—then back to the description of the distressing situation. In typical eastern style, Jonah goes round and round, saying a similar thing but adding new things as he goes on. These are some of the beauties of the eastern culture. Verse 5: "The engulfing waters threatened me, the deep surrounded me; seaweed was wrapped around my head. To the roots of the mountains I sank down; the earth beneath barred me in forever."

We have here a comprehensive description of Jonah's misery. It is very common in the Bible for devout people to recall their past miseries. It may have been a very bitter past, but it is recorded without a sense of bitterness. The bitterness was there, but grace was greater than the bitterness. In the Scriptures the godly often look back to their former bitterness without the spirit of bitterness. They do it as a prelude to describing the marvels of grace. Grace has overcome evil. Bitterness is gone and is replaced by thanksgiving.

Thanksgiving and bitterness cannot coexist. You cannot be thankful and bitter at the same time. When we look back, we say that it was awful, but we quickly add, "But thank God that's the past!" God's goodness was greater than the awfulness.

I wonder, do you look back at your past experiences with bitterness? Let me tell you, my friend, that grace can heal, because grace is greater than your bitter experiences. Let God heal those bitter memories. Sometimes the healing does not take place immediately following your conversion. There may be memories so deep that grace has not yet touched them, and letting those memories surface may be very painful for you. But you can do it, because grace is deeper still.

If you have not experienced the power of grace over your bitter past, let me urge you not to rest until healing has become a reality. Perhaps you should go to someone you respect, so that they can help you apply grace to your bitter memories. Before grace came to Jonah's life, he had to first accept the full implications of his sin. And that's what he did. But when he did that, he was graced.

Look at the second part of verse 6: "But you . . ." But *God*—that's the difference! You may have had this sin or that problem, but God is bigger than your sin and greater than your problem! So verse 4 goes on to say, "Yet I will look again toward your holy temple," and that hope of "yet I" is answered in verse 6 by "But you . . ." *But God* . . . May you see the "But God" in every crisis you face.

That *but* introduces us to the fourth segment of this psalm of praise. First the proclamation, then the introductory summary, then a looking back to the time of need and then a *report of deliverance.* "But you brought my life up from the pit." Here is the turning point in Jonah's testimony. In verse 7 he explains it in greater detail: "When my life was ebbing away . . ." Jonah had come to an utterly desperate situation. But man's extremity is God's opportunity! In his desperate state he says, "I remembered you." Jonah had ignored God, but then in his desperation he turned back to God, he remembered God, and he says, "My prayer rose to you, to your holy temple."

This description of Jonah remembering God at his extremity reminds me of the story of John Newton, author of the hymn "Amazing Grace." He lived a very debased life as a slave trader. Once, when he was in a terrible storm, Newton remembered what he had heard about God and Christ, and he placed his trust in Christ. He had no full understanding of salvation and its implications, but he always regarded that experience in the storm as "the hour I first believed, when a wretch like me was saved."

Shortly after that Newton set sail from England, as second in command on a ship that was going to bring slaves. He had no fellowship on the ship, he slackened in prayer and Bible study, and gradually he backslid. The only difference between him and the others on board ship was that he did not swear. But he was in a weak spiritual state, and in this state the slaves came on board. Each of the sailors chose a girl to abuse, and Newton found he could not resist. He joined the others, and we are told that during the next few months he went down to unbelievable depths of evil and sin.

Nights of debauchery began to weaken him until he got very sick. He got so bad that he thought he'd die. Then and only then did he remember God—first with great fear for God as judge, and then with the realization that God is merciful. Newton returned to God and never backslid violently again. He became a great servant of God and one of the most powerful forces in abolishing slavery from Britain.

Indeed, some come back to God only when they have come to the end of themselves and have nowhere else to go for help. Skeptics say that these desperate cries for help are not genuine. We may disbelieve such prayers and be skeptical, but God always listens to the cries of a sincere soul.

Jacques Ellul has said, "God always takes seriously a cry of a man in distress, a suffering man, a man face to face with death." Ellul goes on to say that what God does not take so seriously is the cold, calculated, rational decision of a person who weighs the odds and condescendingly accepts the hypothesis of God. Such people think they are worthy of God, but the Bible says no one deserves salvation.

Psalm 51:17 says, "The sacrifices of God are a broken spirit; a broken and contrite heart, O God, you will not despise." Listen to Ellul again: "The truth is that God responds not to our better feelings, but to the desperate cry of the man [or woman] who has no other help but God. God responds to the man in trouble who has nowhere to turn." Let's be careful about judging some prayers as being unworthy of salvation.

Some of you may feel you have gone so far from God that there's no hope for you. Take heart! The Bible says that God will not despise a broken and a contrite heart. He heard the prayers of Jonah, he heard the prayers of John Newton, and he can hear your prayer too!

In verses 8 and 9 we see the fifth aspect of this psalm of praise for deliverance: Jonah *praises God for his qualities.* He says in verse 8,

"Those who cling to worthless idols forfeit the grace that could be theirs." Jonah is stating a general principle here regarding God and his ways with people. He says that it is not worth following other gods. Why? First, because they are worthless. They are powerless to help us. Second, by clinging to these idols, we forfeit the grace that could be ours. The glory of the gospel is that there is grace! Other religions have tremendous ethics and great principles, but they do not provide the strength for us to fulfill those principles. Christianity is a religion of grace. God helps us. The last part of verse 9 sums it up by saying, "Salvation comes from the LORD."

I want you to notice something about this particular aspect of the prayer. These two statements in verses 8 and 9 are theological principles that are always true. They are abiding facts about God. These facts provide the raw materials for praise. We see Jonah move from thanksgiving for deliverance to praise for God's attributes.

Can you see the difference between thanksgiving and praise here? We must not base our praise and prayers only on specific incidents. Specific incidents come and go. But while our experiences are varied and changing, the eternal realities of God do not change. We must have a place in our life for these eternal realities. Otherwise Christianity will be based on experience—and experience is a very shaky foundation for life. So while thanksgiving focuses on what has been done in our experience, praise focuses on who God is and how he acts eternally. In our prayer life we need to thank God for what he has done in our experience and praise him for his eternal qualities.

Now we come to the sixth aspect of Jonah's prayer, which is a *renewed vow to praise God.* Look at verse 9: "But I, with a song of thanksgiving, will sacrifice to you. What I have vowed I will make good." Jonah resolves to praise God. This type of resolve is very common in the Bible. These resolves address the will. They are deliberate decisions to praise God.

Sometimes praise does not come naturally to us. Our mood may not be right to praise God. Praise is not always a spontaneous outburst of our experience. Such outbursts may happen after exciting experiences, but we don't have exciting experiences every day. At times we need to address our wills and make a decision to praise God. That may sound like bondage, but it isn't. When we praise God, we are praising him for things that are eternally true. When we start praising God, we will find out that praise was what we wanted to do in our inner self. Our external mood did not spontaneously produce praise, but in our heart of hearts that's what we wanted to do.

Christianity is often like that. When I go to pray, I often don't feel like praying. But I decide to pray anyway, and when I begin praying, I find that I deeply enjoy it!

Christianity is not a drudgery. Don't ever become a missionary because you feel guilty. Get involved in the world evangelization because you want to be obedient to God! When we are obedient to God, we open the door to experiencing his joy fully. When we have opened ourselves to that joy, whatever our trouble or suffering may be, there is a joy that is too deep for any of our troubles to reach. C. S. Lewis said that the whole mark of the Christian is not love, not even faith, but joy—joy because we are living with the King of kings and Lord of lords!

A Song amid the Gloom

How could Jonah have prayed a prayer like this from inside a fish? That's hardly a place to pray a song of deliverance! Some have rejected the idea that this psalm was sung from inside the fish. They say it was probably a later edition inserted in the wrong place by some editor. But is such a mistake probable?

Jacques Ellul points out that Jewish rabbis in the pre-Christian era were characterized by patience, competence, erudition and acuteness. Could such meticulous people have made such a glaring mistake of putting this in the wrong place? To accept this, says Ellul, is to regard the commentators who amended the text as imbeciles. If Jonah could not have prayed like this, the rabbis would have made some adjustments to make the text sound a little less silly. The prayer is there because obviously it is intended to be there.

How then could Jonah have prayed a prayer like this from inside the fish? Verse 1 gives us the key. Jonah prays to the Lord his God. Jonah's relationship with his God has been reestablished. At the end of verse 1 we are told that he had accepted his sinfulness. Now he opens the door for God to come into him, and reestablishes his contact with grace. There is still gloom all around him physically, but a ray of light has crept through the clouds of darkness. That ray of light is, as it were, a guarantee of God's abounding sufficient grace. Jonah clings to that little ray of light. With the eyes of faith, he sees the sunshine of God's grace behind the clouds. Jonah can sing a song of praise in the night because God is who he says he is, and Jonah knows the night will pass.

The same is true for us. When we feel surrounded by darkness, suddenly God will give us a little sense that he is still with us. That little sense is like a light that enters our experience and envelops us with hope. God is! God is still there, and God's grace is greater than every circumstance we face.

The miracle is completed with Jonah's release. Verse 10 states: "And the LORD commanded the fish, and it vomited Jonah onto dry land." The door is open once again for God to work with Jonah, to use him as his prophet.

It is striking that almost all the phrases in this psalm are from the Bible. Jonah's prayer reveals that he had memorized the Scriptures. He didn't have a Bible with him inside the fish, but he had one in his heart. If we want strength from God to face the crises of life, we need to be reading the Scriptures when we don't have the crises, when things are going fine. Psalm 119:11 says, "I have hidden your word in my heart that I might not sin against you." When a crisis comes, we may not have time to go and get a Bible. So God's Word needs to be stored in our hearts—ready for use—like water in a reservoir.

There is no magical formula, however, for memorizing Scripture. It comes through a regular, disciplined study of God's Word. If you have not begun such disciplined study, may you begin it. And if you have begun such study, may you long continue it.

4
Revival in Nineveh
Jonah 3

Ajith Fernando

IN JONAH 2 WE SAW HOW JONAH HAD BEEN RESCUED AND HOW GRATEFUL HE was for being rescued. In Jonah 3 we will see how Jonah is recommissioned and the ministry he carries out as a recommissioned person.

A Second Chance
"Then the word of the LORD came to Jonah a second time" (3:1). Jonah got a second chance. When did this happen? We don't really know. Perhaps it was the moment he set foot on dry land or some time later. We aren't told when, but we are told that he got a second chance.

Not everybody in the Bible gets a second chance. We have stories of prophets, for example, who disobey God and then cannot go back to their ministry. We should not assume we will get a second chance just because Jonah did. The Bible doesn't give us that assurance. So long as we are sensitive to God, we can come back to him. Sometimes, however, we close ourselves to God by our disobedience and thus block our way to restoration. It is dangerous to take chances with disobedience. God is too holy to make it safe for us to take risks with his will. Hebrews 10:31 says, "It is a dreadful thing to fall into the hands of the living God."

But the story of Jonah gives hope to anyone who realizes that he or she has moved away from God's will. If we return to God, he will accept us. Isaiah urges us to "seek the LORD while he may be found; call on him while he is near. Let the wicked forsake his way. . . . Let him turn to the LORD, and he will have mercy on him, and to our God, for he will freely pardon" (55:6-7).

I am reminded of John Sung, the son of a pastor in China. He felt the call to the ministry, and a missionary lady who saw his potential arranged for him to study in the United States. He did brilliantly there, not only in theology but also in science. He earned his Ph.D. in chemistry and received national acclaim. After graduation, numerous opportunities opened up before him, and gradually he gave up thoughts of Christian ministry. He stayed on at Ohio State University, working on a project. But with his disobedience also came restlessness and unhappiness.

One evening as he sat in the moonlight thinking of home, he seemed to hear the voice of God saying, "What shall it profit a man if he gain the whole world and lose his soul?" The very next morning the representative from the Wesley foundation at OSU visited him. One of the first things he said was, "You know, you are not a bit like a scientist. You look more like a preacher!"

Sung ended up in a prestigious theological seminary in New York, although without much of a desire to join the ministry. While he was there, he lost his faith and began to think of evangelical Christianity with scorn.

His misery increased, and he sought refuge in Buddhism and Taoism, chanting their scriptures and following their way of self-denial. Then he tried some of the cults in New York. In deep distress, he happened to go to an evangelistic campaign at Calvary Baptist Church, where he expected to hear a famous preacher. Instead, the speaker was a fifteen-year-old girl! As she spoke, he felt the presence of God in her, and it shocked him. He came back to the next four meetings and began to recover spiritually.

Having returned to God, he was so enthusiastic that people thought he was mentally unbalanced. He was sent to an asylum and was later released only on the condition that he go to China. He went, and what a ministry he had! He became one of Asia's greatest preachers in the first half of this century.

Have you moved away from the place of God's call to you? Come back to him! As long as you're sensitive to his voice, there is hope.

A Difficult Call

In verse 2 the Lord says, "Go to the great city of Nineveh." This is the second time Nineveh has been described as a great city. Again this places emphasis on the immensity of the task before Jonah. This wasn't going to be an easy job. The Bible never downplays the difficult aspects of God's call. It is a glorious call, and with it comes adequate provision, but it is a hard call. Whether you follow Christ into the business world, or whether you're going to the mission field, it's going to be hard.

Consider the call into missionary service. There is the frustration of taking so much time to identify with the people to whom you're ministering. Many, therefore, choose not to identify. There is the disappointment of not being appreciated by the people you have come to serve. There are problems with fellow Christians. Some people who have trouble in their so-called secular jobs decide to go into Christian work because it is so much more pleasant. Well, they're in for a shock! Invariably it is going to be harder. If you want to be a missionary, don't go like a starry-eyed idealist. The shock of reality may be too difficult for you to take. You may go back disillusioned.

John Calvin said that the reason that the character of the city was mentioned "was that Jonah might gird up himself for the contest, so that he might not afterward fail in the middle of his course."

A Message from God

The second part of verse 2 states that the Lord told Jonah to "proclaim to it the message I give you." Jonah was not too happy about this message, but it sparked a tremendous revival. Why? Obviously the people were prepared. Also, there was power in Jonah's message, because God told him to proclaim it.

This is the real romance of missions. We take a message to created people from their Creator. That is the most important thing they need to hear. That is the greatness of missions. We are taking the only message worth hearing to the people of the world—a message from their Creator.

The romance of missions is not the thrill of travel. After some time, you get tired of the sight of a suitcase. It is not the excitement of adventure, because the adventure soon wears off. It is not the joy of harvesting fruit, because some are called to work in unreceptive areas. They are called to open closed doors, to prepare barren fields for the seed. Others will enjoy the fruits of their work. It is not the fulfillment of using our gifts. One of the most beautiful aspects about Christian ministry is to use our gifts, to be useful, to know that God has given us a valuable contribution to make. But soon we realize our own inadequacy. We realize we are jars of clay.

But praise God these jars of clay contain a treasure (2 Cor 4:7). The Creator's message to this bewildered generation is the only hope they have. It is "the power of God for the salvation of everyone who believes" (Rom 1:16). No wonder Paul said that he's not ashamed of the gospel or, to put it positively, that he was excited about the gospel. Our message is a message from God. First Peter 4:11 states: "If anyone speaks, he should do it as one speaking the very words of God."

I work for Youth for Christ. Our primary focus is to proclaim Christ to young people who are out of contact with the church, young people who are not interested in Christianity. We have various types of programs to attract these young people—sports, music, drama, adventure—all sorts of things just to make contact with these non-Christian youth.

At the end of these programs we often preach the gospel, and usually I have the responsibility of doing this. For many of the youth, this is the least important part of the program. Some of them walk away when I start speaking. When I get up to speak, I struggle with nervousness. I often feel like Daniel in the den of lions. But I have a confidence. This is not my message. This is the message of the King of kings and the Lord of lords, the Creator of these young people! This gives me confidence—confidence not in myself, but in the message, because it's the truth that will set these young people free. So let's stay close to the message. Let's know it thoroughly. Let's proclaim it faithfully.

Jonah Obeys

We are told in verse 3 that "Jonah obeyed the word of the LORD and went to Nineveh." As we have seen, obedience is the key to effectiveness. It is a difficult road to follow; there will be problems. But if we obey, God will use us and lead us to victory.

The tremendous way God delivered Jonah would have given him

courage to be obedient. The experience of God's power would have made him confident in launching out on this difficult call. If God could rescue him from the raging seas, he would certainly sustain him in this wicked city.

Each experience of God's provision gives us strength for fresh exploits for God. In fact, it places on us the responsibility to launch out into new depths of obedience. Jonah's salvation from the seas was a blessing. Jonah's call to go to Nineveh was a commission.

Often blessings open doors to commissions. Have you seen God work in your life? Have you seen him answer prayer? Have you seen him guide you through turbulent times? Have you experienced his healing touch on your body? Then if he gives you some new assignment, take heart and follow. The blessing gives us the courage to be obedient.

Preaching Judgment in Nineveh

In verse 3 the author adds a note about the importance of Nineveh: "Now Nineveh was a very important city—a visit required three days." The New American Standard is more literal. It says, "Nineveh was an exceedingly great city, a three day's walk." This statement has provided some material for those who deny the historical reliability of Jonah. Archaeology has revealed that the inner wall of Nineveh was about eight miles long. So why does the author say a visit required three days? Jonah could have completed the trip in much less than a day.

Perhaps the author meant that it took three days to walk through the whole city, or that it took three days to cover the whole administrative district of Nineveh—greater Nineveh. Donald Robinson, who is now the Anglican Archbishop of Sydney and the author of the commentary on Jonah in the New Bible Commentary, points out that the entire circuit of the Nineveh district was sixty-one and a half miles, which would amount to a three day's journey.

"On the first day," verse 4 tells us, "Jonah started into the city. He proclaimed: 'Forty more days and Nineveh will be overturned.' " Starting to preach must have been very difficult. Jonah did not overcome this difficulty by secretly entering the city at night and whispering the message to a few people. We are told that he cried out, he proclaimed. The word suggests a bold proclamation. But once the start was made, the first big hurdle overcome, the news seems to have spread like wild fire. These people who had already been prepared by God came in crowds to hear him.

Let me mention in passing that the same thing happens when we witness to strangers. Often the hardest step is the first one. Very often when I'm traveling in a bus or a train, I know I should talk to the person next to me about Jesus Christ. Getting started is the hardest thing. My heart starts making all sorts of noises, and it is very difficult to begin. But once I've begun, I'm often surprised to see how open people are to the gospel. This isn't always the case, but often you will find it to be true.

"Forty more days," Jonah proclaimed, "and Nineveh will be overturned." Nineveh is given forty days. The word *forty* in the Bible is often associated with judgment and testing. Notice that Jonah's message is a message of judgment. He says, "Nineveh is going to be overturned." Here is a stranger from a small and relatively weak nation, and these are arrogant, powerful Assyrians. It seems quite inappropriate for Jonah to preach judgment. Wouldn't it have been better for him to preach about how important these people were to God? Shouldn't he have told them how much they could achieve if only God were on their side? Wouldn't large crowds have come to hear him if only he had told them how good they were in the sight of God?

It's true that people are important to God. When they are related to him, the possibilities of grace are so big that we cannot even fathom what God can do through them. But first Jonah had to preach a more important message. The Ninevites were selfish people. Their wickedness had gone up before God. They were headed for judgment, and they needed to be told that. So Jonah preached judgment.

Hebrews 6:2 says eternal judgment is one of the basic foundations of Christianity. The writer says we must build on that foundation, but I wonder if we've even laid it! Some say you can preach about judgment to uptight fundamentalists. You can say, "Some of you will go to hell!" and they will respond "Amen, brother!" Others say you can preach about judgment to primitive people living under the fear of the spirits, but not to sophisticated intellectual audiences. But when Paul preached to the Athenians, who were the most sophisticated audience he ever preached to, he preached about judgment (Acts 17:31). His method was philosophical because they were intellectuals, but his message included judgment.

It is interesting that two of the most brilliant minds the western church produced in recent years spent a lot of time reflecting and writing about judgment and hell. I refer to that brilliant American scholar, Jonathan Edwards, and to the great British lay theologian and apologist, C. S. Lewis.

People have brought dishonor to the message of judgment by the way they've preached on hell. They have been unwise, insensitive and disrespectful of their audience. Many have condescendingly dumped accusations at prostitutes and drunks in a way that was an insult to their humanity. In the Bible, judgment is preached not only to prostitutes—they already know they are lost—but also to sophisticated intellectuals who walk about with their noses up in the air. Yet it is done in a way that is appropriate to them, just as Paul did in Athens when he approached the issue of judgment philosophically.

Revival in Nineveh

The response of the Ninevites is surprising: verses 3-9 describe a revival! The word *revival* is used in many ways today. But the specialized use in church history is for a widespread religious awakening, where not one person but large numbers of people take God seriously, confess their sin and get right with God. Usually revival refers to, Christians who are revived and then respond in outreach to non-Christians. In Nineveh, however, those who were revived did not know God.

Verse 3 tells us that the Ninevites believed God. Now many eminent commentators believe that Nineveh's repentance was incomplete. They say that because Jonah's message was incomplete, the Ninevites could not have known enough about the Lord to exercise saving faith. Perhaps Jonah's message was incomplete, or perhaps only the salient features of his message were mentioned. We do not know. I greatly respect the scholars who don't think these people were really converted, but it seems to me that a genuine conversion took place.

The first response mentioned is that they believed God (v. 5). Then we are told that they declared a fast and that all of them, from the greatest to the least, put on sackcloth.

Fasting is a sign of lamentation or sorrow over sin. It is a physical expression of the earnestness of people who are abasing themselves before God. When the Ninevites fasted, it revealed that they were serious about their problem.

Sackcloth was normally worn only by poor, by prisoners or by slaves. By putting on sackcloth, the Ninevites showed that they had become serious about sin. They realized that sin is not something to be trifled with. Repentance is not something cheap, and they refused to ignore the gravity of sin. We see here a real sorrow over sin, a frank admission of guilt.

Unfortunately, guilt has become a bad word in many quarters today. That is what happens when guilt is experienced without the counterexperience of grace. But when there's grace, grace is greater than sin, and guilt becomes the gateway to freedom. We accept our guilt, we confess our sin, we ask God's forgiveness, and then forgiveness is assured. God pronounces us righteous, forgiven, and we are freed from guilt. That's why Jesus said in John 8:36, "If the son sets you free, you will be free indeed."

Some say that all this talk of guilt makes people psychologically sick. Indeed, without grace, guilt can make you psychologically sick. But the opposite is also true. If you refuse to face up to your guilt, you will become psychologically sick. We cannot destroy the reality of guilt by denying it, because we are all sinners. We may suppress it, we may try to forget it, but it works inside of us like a festering wound, while on the outside we look quite clean. Then we will be really sick. So guilt without grace makes us sick, and guilt suppressed makes us sick. But guilt erased by grace makes us whole and free.

These people accepted their guilt before God. Then we are told in verse 6 that the king also repented: "When the news reached the king of Nineveh, he rose from his throne, took off his royal robes, covered himself with sackcloth and sat down in the dust." The king's action, of course, is a real evidence of revival. Instead of sitting on the throne, he sits down in the dust. Instead of wearing his royal robes, he puts on sackcloth. Now this is most unexpected when we realize the power of kings in ancient times. They were absolute monarchs. They made the rules. They were the law. They had no constitution to bind them, no investigative reporters or photographers to hound them.

Today the situation is so different. But even today, often the last thing leaders will do is to admit they are wrong. They will deny the charge. They will put the blame on someone else. They will make life difficult for those who accuse them. They will erase tapes. And they will shred documents.

However, to accept one's faults is the sign of a truly great leader. This is often considered to be a sign of weakness because of our warped sense of values. But for a Christian, God's glory and honor are the most important thing. Sin dishonors God, and when a Christian leader sins, he or she dishonors God. But when a person accepts responsibility for his sin, he upholds God's principles.

By the leader's confession, God's honor is maintained. The leader may be disgraced, but God is held up high. God's principles are honored even in the leader's disgrace. But because the leader upholds God's glory, that disgrace is only temporary. God will honor that leader, for he has honored God by his confession. Honor will surely come— if not here, then most surely in heaven. After all, we are going to spend the rest of eternity in heaven. Why can't we wait until we get to heaven to be honored?

When I was a teenager, I heard a story about the great evangelist D. L. Moody. Evidently, Moody loved his flower garden. One day when he got home, he found that his son had trampled and ruined some of his beautiful plants. Moody lost his temper and was very harsh with his son. After a good scolding and perhaps a spanking, Moody sent his son up to his room.

Shortly afterwards, the son heard his father climbing the stairs— an unmistakable sound, because D. L. Moody weighed three hundred pounds, and the stairs were wooden! The son thought, "Now what's going to happen?" But Moody came to his son and said, "You did wrong, son. But I also did wrong. I lost my temper, and I'm sorry." This great man, who was highly acclaimed worldwide, was humble enough to apologize to his son. The son later reported that this incident did not cause him to dishonor his father, but rather was a big influence in his accepting God in his life.

Throughout the history of revivals, you will see that they were often sparked or accelerated when leaders confessed sin in their lives. Over and over again in the history of revivals, it was the leaders who led in confession. When they were honest, they encouraged others to be honest.

Sometimes leaders pray earnestly for revival, and God shows them that *they* need to be revived. There's a famous revival prayer that says, "Lord, send revival, and let it begin with me." When the leaders lead by walking in the light, others will get serious with God, and they will walk in the light. What does it mean to walk in the light? It means to be honest with ourselves.

It doesn't matter whether you're going to be humiliated, if you want God's glory on your campus or in your country. Be honest with God. If that means you will be disgraced, it doesn't matter. Let God be glorified.

Verse 7 says the king issued a proclamation in Nineveh. "By the decree of the king and his nobles: Do not let any man or beast, herd or flock, taste anything; do not let them eat or drink. But let man and beast be covered with sackcloth."

Here is an official rule, urging expressions of sorrow over sin. Revival has resulted in laws which are conducive to holiness. Indeed, you cannot legislate morality; it must be a choice made by individual people. But the laws of the nation can certainly make it easier for people to follow the path of righteousness.

Sometimes, by refusing to take a stand on moral issues, governments make available to people things which they find difficult to handle in their own strength. Pornography is a good example. We say people must be free to choose on these matters. But after counseling young people who have been enslaved to pornography, I can say that by allowing youth to be exposed to pornography, governments have not affirmed their freedom but have contributed to their enslavement. Young people are powerless to overcome the temptation, though they would like to. Governments have the responsibility to provide an environment conducive to holiness. This law of the king does that.

Note that even animals are included in this repentance. In 4:11 God proclaims his concern for animals as well as people. The book of Jonah presents animals as a significant part of the community of Nineveh.

Throughout history, revivals have contributed to increased concern for animals. Revival makes people become what God intends them to be—truly human. This in turn means they become humane in their behavior toward animals. Proverbs 12:10 states: "A righteous man cares for the needs of his animal." Earle Cairns, in his fine book on the history of revivals called *An Endless Line of Splendor,* points out that the Royal Society for the Prevention of Cruelty to Animals (SPCA) was founded by an Anglican minister, Arthur Broome, with aid from William Wilberforce and his friends. These men were key figures in the great revivals of the eighteenth and nineteenth centuries.

In the second part of the king's proclamation (v. 8), we see what is probably the heart of revival: "Let everyone call urgently on God." All the outward acts mentioned previously find their meaning in this sentence. The people did all these things because they were serious about God. And that is the heart of revival. When people are serious about God, they see how serious their sin is.

The word translated "urgently" is more literally translated in the older translations as "mightily" (ASV, KJV). The root meaning of the Hebrew word is "strength." We are talking about a situation when people seek God with their whole being, when they will not allow anything to stand between them and God.

The great preacher R. A. Torrey used to have as the theme of his evangelistic campaigns: "Get right with God." That's when revival takes place, when people say I must get right with God in every area of my life. God's searchlight must come after me, and I must seek him. There was an old saint who once said, "I have one passion— Jesus."

Most people, however, prefer to take things easy. There is no fire in their dedication. Such people will never see revival come down. I will never forget the founder's day chapel service at Asbury Theological Seminary when I was a student. A great warrior of God in his mid-eighties was the preacher. He told us about the founding president of Asbury Seminary, Henry Clay Morrison. One day while they were praying, Morrison began to get more and more intense in his prayer. Finally, he stood up, looked up into the sky and said, "Oh God, save us from being ordinary!" May God save each of us from having an ordinary relationship with him!

If the previous section of Jonah described the heart of revival, the next section gives the evidence. It says, "Let them give up their evil ways and their violence." The mourning for sin described in verses 5-7 is very important. But as Leslie Allen points out, it also could be "a cultic show of penitence." There must be a change in behavior. I have seen people weep at meetings where there was particularly severe conviction of sin, but after a few weeks I realized that their weeping was induced more by the atmosphere in the meeting than by true inner conviction on their part. There was no long-term change in their behavior.

The history of revival shows that when revival comes, people give up their evil ways. Bars and brothels often close down, either for lack of business or because the owners themselves are converted. For example, after revival hit Asbury College and Seminary, convicted students returned books they had stolen from the seminary bookstore.

People give up not only moral evil but also social evil. The abolition of slavery in England was a direct result of revived people who realized that slavery is incompatible with Christianity.

The Earl of Shaftesbury is a great example of spiritual revival resulting in a passion for social justice. He realized that in England the poor and weak had no hope of improving their lot. They were being exploited, but they did not have the strength to overcome their exploitation. Shaftesbury knew this was evil, so he decided to battle the evil by introducing legislation which protected the poor and the weak. His first struggle was on behalf of the mentally ill. Then he had legislation passed which protected factory workers from exploitation, especially women and children. Next he worked to introduce rules against abuses of chimney sweeps. The Duke of Argyll said, "The social reforms of the past century have not been due to a political party. They have been due to the influence, the character, the perseverance of one man. I refer of course to Lord Shaftesbury."

Yet Lord Shaftesbury was passionately committed to evangelism. He said, "All life is reduced to a transaction between the individual soul and the individual Savior." On another occasion he said, "I believe that the remedy for all our distress is one of the simplest and one of the oldest; the sole sovereign remedy is to evangelize the people by telling them the story of the cross on every occasion and in every place. I believe with all my heart that Christ and he alone is the power of God unto salvation."

Are you committed to Jesus? Are you committed to his principles? Then you must be committed to fighting all forms of evil, both personal and social.

Verse 8 singles out one particular form of evil—violence. How relevant today! Violence is one of the most influential forces in the world today. Violence takes place when an end is pursued with no regard for human life, human welfare and moral law. This, of course, is how the Assyrians achieved their ends. Today many people think that this is the quickest way to get things done. Indeed, you may achieve a short-term goal.

But we know that violence begets violence. Martin Luther King, in his book *Strength to Love,* called this "the chain reaction of evil, resulting in a downward spiral of destruction." Coming from a country which has so much violence, I can say that we Christians must stand up against violence and refuse to condone it as a suitable way to achieve our ends, however just those ends may be.

The king's proclamation concludes by expressing the hope that through God's mercy judgment might be averted. Verse 9 states, "Who knows? God may yet relent and with compassion turn from his fierce anger so that we will not perish." The king does not claim to deserve forgiveness; he only hopes for mercy. And such alone receive mercy, as an old Puritan saying states: "God has two thrones: one in the highest heaven, and the other in the lowliest heart."

Those who thrust themselves on the mercy of God do indeed receive mercy, which is what happens next: "When God saw what they did and how they turned from their evil ways, he had compassion and did not bring upon them the destruction he had threatened" (v. 10).

The words *had compassion* (NIV) are perhaps more accurately translated as "relented" or "repented" in other versions. These words are used when God changes his intended course of action because people change their course of action. When the Ninevites repented, God also repented.

Faithful to Our Call
Jonah 3 has given us a description of revival. Jonah, the agent of revival, was not the greatest model of godliness. He was what someone has called "a reluctant missionary." But he was obedient. He was faithful to his call, and God used him mightily.

That is what we must be. We must pray for revival. We must do all God asks us to do. We must proclaim the Word of God. We must denounce sin. We must demonstrate the love of Christ by our lives. We do all these things knowing that God will act in the way he knows best. We leave the results to him and do all we know to do. D. L. Moody once said, "Pray as if everything depended on God, and work as if everything depended on you."

God will send revival when he knows the time is ripe for it. But one thing we can do is to make sure we are in a revived state and obeying God in everything. Our prayer should be: "Lord send revival, and let it begin with me!"

5
God's Concern for Nineveh
Jonah 4

Ajith Fernando

IN JONAH 3 WE SAW THE GREAT REVIVAL IN NINEVEH. REVIVALS ARE A TIME OF rejoicing. Psalm 85:6 says, "Will you not revive us again, that your people may rejoice in you?" If God uses a preacher as an instrument of revival, the preacher is usually the one who is most elated. It brings a person deep joy to be the chosen instrument of God for a special task.

Chapter 4 begins with one of the most profound words in the Bible—"But." *But* always introduces a change in direction. It indicates that something unexpected has happened. There are glorious *buts* in Scripture, but this is an inglorious *but*. Verse 1 says, "But Jonah was greatly displeased and became angry." God has miraculously worked, but the instrument of God's action is angry.

Verse 2 continues, "He prayed to the LORD." What follows doesn't sound like a prayer. It's actually a complaint. But it's a complaint which takes the form of a prayer. In the Bible we often find great servants of God complaining directly to God. The Bible never glorifies these complaints nor even justifies them. In fact, the complainer is often rebuked, although the rebuke is sometimes very gentle. It is foolish to doubt God's wisdom and his sovereignty. But if we do doubt God's ways, it is best to face up to the reality of that doubt and go directly to God with our problem. That's what Jonah did. When we go to God with our anger, we give him an opportunity to respond to our questions.

God responded to Moses when he complained about the burdens of leadership (Num 11). He responded to Jeremiah when he complained about his loneliness (Jer 15). He responded to the psalmist Asaph when he complained about the prosperity of the wicked in contrast to his own failures (Ps 73). He responded to Jonah when he complained about his theological problem. Each of these responses gives us deep insights into the ways of God, because God answers their complaints. So while we can fault Jonah for his attitude, we can at least commend him for his honesty and for expressing his doubt.

Some orthodox people are afraid to be honest about their doubts. They won't grapple with their doubts. They just suppress them. But when you suppress your doubts, you often become intellectually defensive, stiff, superficial. Often you become unreal.

Jonah was honest about his doubts, and because God is supreme, he was not intimidated by Jonah's doubt. In fact, God gave Jonah an answer that was a deep revelation of truth. The doubt opened the way to deeper knowledge.

A deep experience of God often comes from struggle. The reason there are so many shallow people today is because they have avoided struggle. They have opted for quick solutions. And because they have opted for quick solutions, they never find the deep truths of God. Those who face up to their doubts, who go to God with those doubts and who wrestle with him about them will emerge with a deeper and surer faith.

Rejecting God's Mercy

Notice Jonah's prayer in verse 2: "Oh LORD, is this not what I said when I was still at home? That is why I was so quick to flee to Tarshish." Finally we discover the reason for Jonah's disobedience in chapter one. Why did he flee to Tarshish? Why is he angry now? "I knew that you are a gracious and compassionate God, slow to anger and abounding in love, a God who relents from sending calamity." Jonah was revolting against God extending his mercy to Gentiles.

Jonah's prayer is based on a common Jewish creed which is often quoted in the Old Testament. (For example, it is found in Exodus 34:6-7.) The key phrase in the creed is "abounding in love." The Revised Standard Version translates it as "steadfast love." The New American Standard renders it as "loving kindness." This is one of the most beautiful words in the whole Bible. The Hebrew word is *hesed,* which is often used to describe God's covenant love with Israel.

The word emphasizes God's *loyalty* to Israel. It stresses that he will be faithful to his covenant. But many Jews regarded *hesed* as a privilege reserved only for them. They did not want God to extend it to others. When God asked Jonah to go to Nineveh, he suddenly realized that God intended to show his *hesed* to the Gentiles. Jonah thought that *hesed* should only be given to those who deserve it. And the Jews, according to Jonah's way of thinking, deserved this loyal love of God.

But in the Bible the word *hesed* is very closely linked with mercy. In fact, the King James Version translates *hesed* as "mercy" most of the time. Because God is merciful, he extends his covenant love to Israel. They don't deserve it. They don't merit salvation. God in his mercy has reached out to them. But when God reaches out to the Ninevites, Jonah revolts.

He is guilty of theological racism. I come from a country torn by racism, and I have observed that racism is one of the last areas the process of sanctification touches in many people's lives. It is shocking to see how many evangelical believers who say they're not racist have feelings of ill will toward those of other races and view them as inferior. That is racism.

What was the reason for Jonah's theological racism? He had forgotten mercy. He had forgotten that he did not deserve salvation. Ephesians 2:8 puts this beautifully. "It is by grace you have been saved, through faith—and this not from yourselves, it is the gift of God." In Romans and Galatians, Paul is at pains to show that even in the Old Testament salvation was by grace. Nobody deserved salvation. Grace is God's free gift, and faith is acceptance of that gift. We don't have to do anything for our salvation except to repent and accept him as Savior and Lord. So often people claim that other things are necessary for salvation—baptism or circumcision or whatever. But they are misinterpreting the Scriptures.

Jonah thought that the Jews deserved their salvation and the Ninevites did not. But Paul goes on to say in Ephesians 2:9 that it is "not by works, so that no one can boast." When people try to earn their salvation, they have an occasion for boasting. They think they are more deserving than others. So when so-called terrible sinners receive salvation, they say, "That's not fair!"

That is how the elder brother responded to the prodigal son. He was angry like Jonah was angry. When the father questioned him about his anger, he said: "All these years I've been slaving for you and never disobeyed your orders" (Lk 15:29). His was a works-righteousness. He didn't know the joy of sonship. All he knew was the drudgery of slavery. People like that are very insecure about their salvation because deep down they know they can't save themselves. They have to keep comparing themselves with others to feel that they are all right.

So someone who understands grace is not like that. He says, "I don't deserve to be saved, but God showed me mercy. Praise God!" That's how Paul felt. In 1 Timothy 1:15-16 he says, "Christ Jesus came into the world to save sinners—of whom I am the worst. But for that very reason I was shown mercy." After contemplating God's mercy, Paul gets so excited that he bursts forth into praise to God: "To the King eternal, immortal, invisible, the only God, be honor and glory for ever and ever. Amen." He was so thrilled that Jesus had showed him mercy!

When we understand grace, our hearts overflow with thanksgiving. Grace also results in the love of God flooding into our hearts. This combination of thanksgiving and love flooding into our hearts bursts forth in evangelism. We are so grateful that we want others to know about God. Christ's love in us drives us and compels us to tell others about the salvation we have.

Billy Bray was a great Methodist lay preacher in England. As a non-Christian, he had no illusions of being a great person who merited salvation. In fact, he was a drunkard who lived a dissipated life. Then he was converted while reading John Bunyan. After his conversion, his life was completely transformed. He remained poor and worked among his fellow miners, enduring much hardship. These miners were violent, sinful people, but they could not resist the power of his preaching and his concern for them. Many were converted through his ministry.

Billy Bray was a huge brute of a man. Sometimes he would go to a home and find out that someone in that home had been converted. He would get so excited that he would take the person, put him on his shoulder, go outside the house and run around praising God. Now we might find that to be a little unusual, but he was a miner. And there's nothing in the Bible that says a miner must give up his mining culture when he comes to Christ. He knew that he did not merit salvation, but he received it because of mercy. So when somebody else came to Christ, he was thrilled.

Now Jonah was wrong in thinking the Jews merited salvation. But he was also wrong in thinking that the Ninevites did not deserve God's mercy. This attitude is common even today. Often we regard people we dislike as unworthy of salvation. In our Youth for Christ ministry in Sri Lanka, much of our work has been with poor people. The hardest group we have tried to reach is the urban slum dwellers. These people have a lot of common vices, so they are disdained by society. (The vices of the rich are far more subtle, but they are just as abhorrent to God.) It has been very hard working with these people. We've seen a lot of failure, disappointment, heartaches, betrayal and dishonesty. Many people have told us that these are dishonorable people, and it's no use working with them. The implication is that they don't deserve salvation.

I believe there is a similar problem among those working with the urban poor in this country. A Christian leader once told me he can't get money from certain foundations for work they do with the urban poor. He found it was easier to get funds for work with middle-class or rich people. The implication is that the urban poor are not worth spending so much money and energy on. You get quicker results with middle-class people.

The best answer we can give to that attitude is found in Romans 5:8, "God demonstrates his own love for us in this: While we were still sinners, Christ died for us." God didn't wait until we became worthy of salvation, because he knew that we didn't have the ability to become worthy. So Christ died for us so that we might be saved. Now that we have experienced salvation, we refuse to say that anyone is beyond salvation, whether they are rich or poor, black or white, yellow or brown. Whether they live in a mansion or in a ghetto, whether their lifestyle is that of a socialite or a violent criminal, they are all within the reach of grace. All can be saved, because grace comes through mercy. Such thinking was foreign to Jonah, so he complained about God showing mercy to the wicked Ninevites.

Jonah Wants to Die
Jonah's statement in verse 3 gives us a bigger shock. He prays, "Now, O LORD, take away my life, for it is better for me to die than to live."

He wants to die. This is the despair of a person whose theology is correct or orthodox, but whose personal desires clash with what he knows to be the will of God. In Hebrew, the words *I, me* and *my* appear nine times in verses 2 and 3. Jonah had the right theology, but he was self-centered. His selfishness caused his attitudes to be warped. His heart and his head were at loggerheads. His heart said, "I and my people are better than other people because we deserve to be saved." His head said, "Salvation is an unmerited gift given because of God's mercy, and so the Ninevites need to hear it just like the Israelites."

There was a conflict within him. He had lost his peace, that *shalom* which the Bible presents as the glorious heritage of those who belong to God. When those who are orthodox disobey God, they are sometimes more miserable than those who don't know the truth. The orthodox know how powerful God is. They know they can't fight him, but in their heart they don't want to follow his ways. What a desperate situation to be in—to know the truth and still not want to follow it, to know the terrible danger of being opposed to God and still not want to agree with him. Such a conflict sometimes becomes so unbearable you come to the point where you think it would be better to die than to live. You become suicidal. And suicide is the ultimate expression of despair.

The Lord replies to Jonah, "Have you any right to be angry?" The word translated as "right" is closely related to the word *better* in verse 3. Both words have the idea of "good." Jonah says, "It is good for me to die." The Lord replies, "Is it good for you to be angry?" Of course, neither is good. In a gentle way, the Lord questions and condemns Jonah's attitude.

The Growth and Destruction of the Vine
Verse 5 says, "Jonah went out and sat down at a point east of the city. There he made himself a shelter, sat in its shade and waited to see what would happen to the city." This shelter must have been a temporary shelter, probably made out of branches and leaves that Jonah found there. It was obviously inadequate, because he was quite unhappy until God provided him with a vine. .

We are told that Jonah sat and waited to see what would happen to the city. Why does he do this? Was he still hoping that God would judge and destroy Nineveh? Was he still waiting for some action from God which would explain his ways more clearly? We are not told the answers to those questions.

Verse 6 tells us that "the LORD God provided a vine and made it grow up over Jonah to give shade to his head to ease his discomfort." The word *provided* appears many times in this book. It's the same word which is found in 1:17, which says that God *provided* a fish to save Jonah. Now he *provides* a vine to make him comfortable.

What is this plant? Verse 10 says it sprang up overnight. This may be literally true, in which case a miracle has taken place. Or the mention of it springing up overnight may be the figure of speech we call a hyperbole. If so, it is a way of describing rapid growth. Some have identified this vine as a *Ricinus communis,* the castor oil plant which grows very fast—but we can't be sure.

Verse 6 tells us that "Jonah was very happy about the vine." This is a very strong response. The NIV is a bit mild here. Leslie Allen translates it as "terribly pleased." The NASB has "extremely happy." In Hebrew the same adverb is used here as in verse one. So in verse 1 Jonah is "terribly upset." In verse 6 he is "terribly pleased." Jonah is having a roller-coaster type of emotional response. He is terribly upset when the Gentiles are saved and terribly pleased when he is looked after.

Why such extreme reactions? My beloved teacher, Daniel Fuller, said: "Jonah regarded [the vine] as an acknowledgment of his inherent worth." When the vine came up, Jonah seemed to say: "I deserve God's help. Here is the evidence that God loves me. This is the way he should treat me." But those trusting in themselves, who think they have inherent worth, are trusting in something very insecure. When they feel affirmed, they respond with great joy. But when they see others affirmed, they cry out "Not fair!" like the brother of the prodigal son.

Two girls were walking along the street one day, and someone met them on the way, coming from the opposite direction. The person looked at one of the girls and said, "You look very beautiful today." The other girl was immediately baptized with a lemon-juice smile. For the rest of the day she was a sourpuss because her friend was affirmed and she was not.

Jonah's extreme reactions show the insecurity of one whose confidence and trust is in himself and not God. Those who trust in God have a quiet confidence, for their hope is not based on their abilities but on God's mercy and care. Isaiah 26:3-4 says, "You will keep in perfect peace him whose mind is steadfast, because he trusts in you.

Trust in the Lord forever, for the LORD, the LORD, is the Rock eternal."

Jonah's joy is short-lived. Verse 7 says that at dawn the next day God provided a worm that chewed the vine so that it withered. What is happening here? Suddenly a vine comes up, and suddenly it withers. God is using a method called the acted parable to get through to Jonah. Sometimes people are so hardened to truth that God can only get through to them by an unusual means.

God did this often in the Old Testament. Once he got a prophet to take a pot and walk around the city. The people thought this was very strange, so they all followed him. When the crowd had all gathered around him, they would not listen to his preaching, so the Lord asked the prophet to take the pot and throw it to the ground. He did so and said, "That's what God is going to do if you don't repent." They would not listen, and so God had to use an acted parable.

Again we find this same word *provide* in verse 7. In 1:17 God provided a fish to save Jonah. In 4:6 God provided a vine to shelter Jonah. Now God provides a worm to discipline Jonah and to teach him a lesson through the extreme discomfort he will shortly have to endure.

These uses of the word *provide* are related to a key theme of this book—God's holy love. God is both loving and holy. He not only blesses people with what they regard as good things. Sometimes God blesses people with chastisement or discipline. He allows us to experience discomfort, pain or heartache to teach us a lesson or to burn off impurities in our lives.

Discipline is one of the clearest examples of God's holy love. Proverbs 3:12 says, "The LORD disciplines those he loves, as a father the son he delights in." Hebrews 12:6 also quotes that verse with approval. First John 4:8 says, "God is love." But this love is not a weak, sentimental, soft love. It is holy love, tough love. Verse 8 presents God's discipline of Jonah at its peak when it says, "When the sun rose, God provided a scorching east wind"—again the word *provided*—"a scorching east wind, and the sun blazed on Jonah's head so that he grew faint."

A recently published book called *The World of the Bible* describes what this scorching east wind is like. It is a dry, hot, desert wind called a sirocco that usually lasts for three to seven days. Normally the humidity of the Middle East is very, very low—forty to seventy-five per cent. During a sirocco, it can drop a further thirty per cent, so it becomes extremely dry. With that drop in humidity also comes a rise in temperature. The air is full of fine dust which blurs the sun, and the dryness makes it wearisome and unbearable. Dennis Bailey says, "It is very trying to the temper and tends to make even the mildest of people irritable and fretful and ready to snap at one another for apparently no reason at all." This is what Jonah had to encounter.

Normally when a sirocco comes people run for shelter. But Jonah's shelter is gone. The only place he could go was back to Nineveh—but he was not about to return there! His situation is desperate. He gets very weak, and we are told that he grows faint. In verse 8 we read that Jonah "wanted to die, and said, 'It would be better for me to die than to live.' " He is totally defeated. Earlier he wanted to die because God had treated Gentiles the way he expected God to treat the Israelites. Now he wants to die because God is treating him the way he expects God to treat the Gentiles. You can imagine Jonah's frustration! He has a stubborn heart, and God is trying to reach out to him. Jonah is brought to the end of himself before he is taught the great lesson of this book.

God Expresses Concern for Nineveh

God questions Jonah again, as he did in verse 4: "But God said to Jonah, 'Do you have a right to be angry about the vine?' 'I do.' he said. 'I'm angry enough to die.' " Jonah is snapping back at God. But God's answer is so typical of God. He does not rebuke the prophet for his attitude. He knows how much Jonah can handle. So instead of rebuking him, he gently but firmly begins to reason with Jonah.

This gentle firmness is seen very often in the Bible when God speaks to his discouraged servants. We see it in God's dealings with Moses, Jeremiah and Elijah when they complained. God disciplines us, but he does so wisely. He knows how much we can take and what's best for us. He never lowers his standards with us. But he varies his tone without varying his demands.

In verse 10 the Lord says, "You have been concerned about this vine, though you did not tend it or make it grow. It sprang up overnight and died overnight." God wants to stress to Jonah that he had 'no deep tie with the vine which withered. He did nothing for it. "He had no investment" in it, as Kohlenberger says. It came up suddenly and died suddenly. Yet Jonah seems to be concerned for this vine.

God then goes on to say that his relationship with Nineveh is far more serious than Jonah's relationship with the vine: "But Nineveh has more than a hundred and twenty thousand people who cannot

tell their right hand from their left, and many cattle as well. Should
I not be concerned about that great city?" God describes the Ninevites
as a people in need. They cannot tell their right hand from their left.
That is, they don't know the truth. They don't know where to go. They
are not innocent, but they are ignorant. God is concerned for them,
not because of their inherent worth but because of their need.

Because they are needy people, God responds with concern and
asks, "Should I not be concerned about that great city?" The word
that the NIV translates as "concerned" has the idea of compassion
or pity. The emphasis is on the helplessness of the Ninevites. This
brings us to the heart of the gospel. We are helpless, under the power
of sin. We have no hope, no ability to save ourselves. But God looked
down on us in mercy and provided a way for our salvation.

Have you been saved? Then you know God is a compassionate
God. If God is compassionate, there is hope for everyone. And if there
is hope for everyone, you should be involved in proclaiming the gospel to those who don't know about it. God is a missionary God. His
followers, therefore, must be missionary people.

This is one of the great arguments for missions. Robert E. Speer,
the great lay missionary leader of the Presbyterian church in this
country, said: "The supreme arguments for missions are not found in
specific words. It is in the very being and character of God that the
deepest ground of the missionary enterprise is to be found. We cannot think of God except in terms which necessitate the missionary
idea." God is concerned for the lost. People are in need, and we are
God's instruments. We must flesh out God's concern by our own
involvement. Henry Martyn, who is one of my heroes, put it beautifully: "The spirit of Christ is the spirit of missions. The nearer we get
to him the more intensely missionary we must become."

The Book of Jonah ends without telling us Jonah's response to
God's teaching. That is an approprate way to end this series of studies. You, too, have been faced with the missionary challenge. Will you
be an agent of God's concern for the lost? Will you give your life for
it? If so, you will begin to share God's concern. And when you share
God's concern, your heart begins to beat with the heartbeat of God.

---

*Ajith Fernando, author, national director of Youth for Christ in Sri
Lanka and a member of the Lausanne Committee for World Evangelization, has an international expository ministry.*

III
The Call
of the
City

6
Overcoming the Real Barriers to Urban Evangelization

Ray Bakke

BILLY GRAHAM RIGHTLY REMINDS US THAT THE CALL TO MISSIONS IS A PERSONAL call. But God does not give us mere advice, which we paternalistically deliver to the city, but news, news that liberates and sets people free from bondage. The fundamental difference between the messages of Jesus Christ and Ann Landers is precisely this. Advice requires you to do something to make things work. News declares what God has already done for you in Jesus Christ. We go forth as persons called by a risen Christ to announce good news.

We have just been reminded by our lucid Sri Lankan expositor Ajith Fernando that God himself is a missionary. God is striving to enlarge our message and get his messengers to enlarge their maps. The mission of Jonah was to go to a city that was filled with hatred and war. The message of Jonah confronts the narcissism of America, and it confronts the ethnocentric gospels which we wrap in flags and deliver to nations around the world.

World-Class Barriers to Urban Mission
My task is to enlarge your map. I want to draw your attention to the

shifting frontiers of mission today. I want to talk about a world that has gone from a world of nations to a world of interconnected multinational cities. It is a world of some 223 nations that is in reality a world of 300 world-class cities, a world growing so fast that by the year 2000 there will be nearly 500 cities of more than 1 million people. The barriers to mission and evangelism today are real and complex.

One of the barriers is simply the demographics. The United Nations has a department of 40 people that focuses on the demographics of cities. And the numbers are staggering. In the next few moments a hundred babies will be born in the world. Forty-nine will be yellow. Thirteen will be white like me. The rest will be black and brown. Most of them will live in the cities of the world.

In order to get to Urbana, most of you passed through metropolitan Chicago, a six-county area with 7.1 million people. I am here to tell you that the monthly net growth of the world is more than the population of metropolitan Chicago. We are talking about a world of rapidly increasing numbers. There have not been a billion minutes since Jesus walked on this earth over nineteen hundred years ago, but we are going to produce a billion-and-a-half new babies in the next thirteen or fourteen years. And without a doubt most of them will live in the cities.

For two thousand years we have had the Great Commission to go into all the world to preach the gospel to all peoples and make disciples of the nations. Now we know where they are—in my neighborhood, in the cities, in Los Angeles, in Miami and the teeming cities around the world. The numbers are staggering—but so is the kaleidoscopic complexity of the cities. The city is like an escalator moving in the wrong direction—like a gigantic magnet sucking people from the jungles, from islands, from tribal groups.

For centuries western Europe could organize its life, its ideology, its world view around the Mediterranean. If you read Henri Pirenne's classic *Medieval Cities,* you will discover that Europe swung for 800 years like a slowly swinging door. She was pushed by Islam and pulled by the northern cities of Germany. Europe was forced to be a nation looking north and west. We have been in an Atlantic-perimeter world for the last 500 to 600 years. But now within this century, your lifetime and mine, the world is swinging again. The door is opening, only this time much faster, and we're shifting from an Atlantic to a Pacific-perimeter world. This new world is beckoning us with explosive and complex cities.

The fastest growing cities in the world are in Latin America, Africa and Asia, and they are changing the way we think, live and construct our economies. Sadly, the fastest growing cities are often in areas where the church is the weakest—in the Asian perimeter. So the scale of urban mission is measured not only by the size and number of the cities, but also by the changing configuration and complexity of the cities.

For example, Mexico City is the oldest city in this hemisphere, but it is also the youngest. Twenty million people live in that city—try to imagine it—twenty million people. But while the median age in Chicago is 31, the median age in Mexico City is 14. That means there are some ten million people in Mexico City under 14 years of age. It is an old city and a young city.

A few weeks ago I was walking the streets of Toronto with a former student of mine, now a missionary to the streets of that city. We were looking at some of the 20,000 teenagers on the streets of Toronto. And as we looked we wanted to weep. Two weeks ago I was in Hollywood, observing some of the 5,000 teenagers on the streets of that city, selling their bodies. They have come from all over, drawn by a dream, but living on the streets.

A few weeks ago I heard the Ecumenical Night Ministry in Chicago tell the story of 10,000 teenagers on the streets of Chicago. They are a city within a city. Thirty per cent of them are psychiatric mental cases, patients who were released from mental institutions and psychiatric hospitals when they lost funding.

The complexity of the city is that it isn't one city. It's a commercial city. It's an industrial city. It's a nocturnal city. It's a daytime city. It's an ethnic city. It's an international city. It's a migrant city. It's a student city. It's a five-star hotel city. It's a derelict city, a deviant city, an institutionalized city. People are being packaged in cities. To reach them is to deal with numbers, growth and complexity.

But many of these cities are not easily accessible to us. Thirty of the cities with populations of more than one million are in China. At least twenty of them are in the Soviet Union. Many of the fastest-growing cities in the world are in the Islamic world. Some are like Beirut, which may be a parable of the city. Today we know it as a violent city. But it is not well known that a decade ago, when the civil war began in Beirut, the population was one million. Today, after years of war and many, many deaths, the population of Beirut is about 1.8 million. In other words, the very pain and struggle of the city have served as a magnet to draw people out of south Lebanon into that city—and it's almost impossible for us to go in and do anything about that.

Personal Barriers to Urban Mission

So when we talk about urban mission today, we are talking about some barriers that are very real. But I want to talk about three barriers that I believe confront you personally. And it seems to me that these are the real barriers.

In 1980 the Lausanne Committee for World Evangelization held a conference in Thailand. My assignment was to help organize the urban part of that consultation. In the preparation we carried on correspondence with people in over a hundred cities. So I carried with me about 5,000 pages of primary research to that conference. We sat down with 110 people who were from six continents and began to look at what God was doing in the cities. We were amazed to find how little was being done by evangelicals and how few mission agencies seemed concerned about preparing missionaries for urban mission. We were also stunned by how God was using new means, new forms and new wineskins.

After that conference I was assigned to travel to about a hundred cities, holding consultations with people, taking a fresh look at their city and ministries on the one hand, and then asking, What are the new models of ministry that are needed to reach this city—whether it be Cairo, Copenhagen, Zagreb or Mexico City?

I had been taught in seminary by the late Paul Little that if people don't come to Christ or won't witness for Christ, it is because they lack two things—either information or motivation. But I'm here to say, there is a third factor in urban mission: *intimidation,* the we-never-did-it-that-way-before syndrome. Those are the seven last words of the church.

The Theological Barrier

One of the barriers is not external in the big, bad city, but internal. It is a theological barrier. Most of us have a personal theology, a personal conversion. I would call it a Philippian theology—a theology of Christ who left the heavens and came down to live within us. A "my God and I" relationship—and it's wonderful. It's pietism. Most of us lack, however, a Colossian theology of a transcendent Christ, who is Lord of the systems and structures of the world, including those gigantic macrostructures of the metroplace, the city. And without that Colossian perspective, we have relief theology, but no theology of reform.

We deal with victims, but we can't deal with the issues of justice. A thief-on-the-cross theology—just enough to make it to heaven—is a place to start. But if we are to engage in urban mission, we are going to have to keep studying. In the words of Walter Scott, "For a Christian one book is enough, but a thousand aren't too many." It is a fact that with the Bible School training which I have, I could be the most educated person in many a village, but in many cases the city will not yield to minimalist education. Some of you will need to go on and study hard to apply that Colossian theology. To personal theology you need to add a public theology of mission. We need not only a missiology of the city, but a biblical theology of the city.

To think biblically means to understand how God has moved in creation and redemption throughout biblical history. To think historically is to understand that the same Spirit of God that moves us today has also led God's people across cultures for the past two thousand years. We need these lessons from history because the city is a museum of art and architecture, a museum of cultures and peoples who come from the far corners of the globe and are being reshaped by the forces of the city.

The voice you hear is in Chicago, but the culture is from some place else. The agendas people carry are from other places. So we need to develop a world view that helps us see that the world now lives in my neighborhood. There are sixty nations represented in my neighborhood in Chicago, sixty nations in the public school where my kids went, and the school teaches in eleven languages. Thirty-five per cent of the neighborhood is Black, but many Black cultures are represented: tobacco culture, cotton culture, coal culture, Caribbean culture. These are all Black cultures, but they are all different. Twenty-eight per cent are Asians, but they are all different. There are north, south and east Asians—some of them are refugees and poor, but many are wealthy and elite.

One of the real barriers to urban missions is the way we have read the Bible as a rural book. We sing "Work for the Night Is Coming" and "I Come to the Garden Alone"—hymns imbued with pastoral and rural imagery. But, as Bill Pannell says, it is very difficult for the urbanite in downtown Cleveland to think in terms of herding sheep.

We need to expand our theology until it encompasses God's vision for the city.

The Ecclesiastical Barrier

Another major barrier is ecclesiastical. For many of us the church has been a club—my white, middle-class church could not survive when the neighborhood changed. Many of us are the product of the white-flight, white-fright syndrome. We fled the city just when God brought the whole world there.

Some of us feel guilty about that. But let me tell you, when you left the city, the Spirit didn't leave. He just jumped into other wineskins. Today the fastest growing churches are often Black, Hispanic or Korean—and many of them worship in languages other than English. The Lord doesn't need you to come back to Chicago as a Messiah sent to save the city. If you come, you must join him in the work he is already doing there.

Today denominations and mission boards are struggling to understand how they should divide the turf. Whereas in the past they could distinguish between home mission and foreign mission, today those distinctions don't make much sense—what is home and what is foreign cannot be so easily distinguished. The Southern Baptist Home Mission ministers in twenty-six languages in Los Angeles alone. The archdiocese of Chicago must deal with twenty-two languages. The foreign field has come home.

Today we need to think in terms of mission to the geographically distant—that mission to reach a billion or more people living far from any existing church—and the new frontier of mission to the culturally distant—that two-and-a-half billion people that live within the shadows of existing churches. We will still need missionaries to cross oceans, mountains and deserts to reach unreached peoples. But the new frontier is in the cities constructed from the mass migrations and exploding birth rates of our day. This is the new reality of world mission.

One of the assignments I enjoy giving to classes on urban mission is to take them into a supermarket and give them thirty minutes to observe what is happening in the neighborhood. They come out and tell me how the food business has changed in the last thirty, even fifteen years. Stores are open twenty-four hours. Everything has been computerized. Prices have gone up. While stores used to carry eight thousand products, they now stock twenty-four thousand products. They have an Asian section, a Spanish section, a Geritol section, a salt-free section. Other sections cater to microwave people. They have foreign-language checkers, and their check-cashing service is more convenient than my bank. Gone are days when the meatcutters union could say "We will not sell meat after six o'clock."

But then I take my students over to a nearby church, and we look at the sign. And what do we see? Morning worship: 11:00 A.M.—as it was in the beginning, is now and ever shall be, world without end.

And I ask, How can a supermarket without the Spirit of God do what the church doesn't seem to be able to do with the Spirit? How can we liberate the church to reach the city? How can we persuade the foreign board to team up with the home board in teaching the crosscultural skills we now need at home? How can we do that? For most of us this is a greater barrier than Islam—and I say that from my own experience of trying to overcome the barrier.

The Fear Barrier
The third barrier is intensely personal—it has to do with our fear of the city. My cousin Gordon went to Zambia. We entered Moody Bible Institute together thirty-one years ago, and he went to Zambia. He is a hero. He is a missionary, and he's got pythons and cobras in his garden. I've got news for him: I've got Pythons and Cobras and Latin Kings in my yard.

But many people who admire my cousin Gordon think I'm stupid to raise my family in the city. There is a dichotomy in the minds of many of us as we think about the city. Many of the great missionary heroes buried their children in foreign lands. But if you take your children to the city today, someone is going to tell you that you are abusing them. You are going to alienate them from the mainstream of our culture. I have heard this argument, and I reject it.

Jesus Christ is Lord of the city. We desperately need families in the city. We need children, for they quickly adapt to the culture and give us access to the culture of the city. They give us reasons to be involved in the schools. We need Christians back in public housing projects, back in the labor unions, back in the playgrounds and grammar schools. We can't afford to pull them out.

We cannot fight the battle for the cities the way we fought the war in Vietnam. We parked our planes on Guam, flew them at 37,000 feet, bombed people to hell, went back for a night's sleep and lost the war. You cannot blitz the cities and expect to win the battle. We have to incarnate the gospel, wrap it up and deliver it in person to the street. The personal challenge is a barrier for many of you. Jonah found it a barrier.

The theme this week is "Should I Not Be Concerned?" Are you concerned enough to overcome the barriers? The numbers are staggering. David Barrett, who knows the numbers better than anyone else, has been telling us that the figures are astounding. Humanly and mathematically speaking, we are losing the battle for the city. I say that apart from what the Spirit of God might do and how you might figure in those numbers. The complexity of the city is overwhelming, and the stunning reality is that the bigger a city gets, the less we can comprehend and communicate that complexity. Social psychologists speak of this as the psychology of overload.

The sheer complexity of the city is staggering, not to speak of the Beiruts, the Sowetos and Nicosias that are locked behind restrictive national borders. But I would remind you of the three barriers you need to confront this week. First, you need to overcome the theological barrier, that seven-foot hump between your personal faith and the faith that equips you for the full-orbed mission of the church in the world of today.

Second, you need to get over the ecclesiastical barrier that looks at the church as a little club and start asking hard questions about how we build churches within the complex structures and ethnicity of our cities. How can the church at home become the foreign church, and how can we speak with integrity about the global mission of the local church in a world in which the nations have come to live with us?

And finally you need to confront the personal issues. You will always be a minority in the city—racially, spiritually, ideologically, politically and almost every other way. Are you ready? Remember Romans 8:31: "If God is for us, who can be against us?" Go for it. Go for it, and God bless you.

Ray Bakke, author of The Urban Christian *(IVP), is professor of ministry at Northern Baptist Theological Seminary and senior and associate international coordinator for the Lausanne Committee for World Evangelization.*

7
The
Streets of
Amsterdam

Floyd McClung, Jr.

I HAVE BEEN LIVING AND WORKING WITH MY WIFE AND OUR TWO CHILDREN IN the city of Amsterdam with Youth With A Mission for the last fourteen years. We live in the red-light district of Amsterdam, which is twelve blocks long and six blocks wide. There are sixteen thousand prostitutes who live and work in that neighborhood and twelve thousand drug addicts. There are also six thousand male prostitutes. In fact, Amsterdam is one of the gay capitals of Europe.

When we moved into the red-light district, two doors to the right of us was a Satanist church. Four doors to the right of us was a homosexual brothel. And two doors to the left of us was a twenty-four-hour porno cinema. We didn't write home about our neighbors very often.

The original purpose my wife Sally and I had in coming to Amsterdam was to work with alienated young people. We started a halfway house, but not long after we arrived, we became concerned for the entire city. One of the first things I did was to walk the streets to try to get a feel for the city, to get to know it, to get God's heartbeat for the city. I once heard Billy Graham say that if he ever started a ministry anywhere in a city, he would spend six months walking its streets getting to know the people and the neighborhoods and praying. I took that advice literally.

As I began to walk the streets and to pray for the people, I became acquainted with the various neighborhoods and people groups. It was an overwhelming and daunting experience. There was neighborhood after neighborhood of high-rise apartment buildings. The city of Amsterdam has about 2.5 million people in the metropolitan area and about eight hundred thousand in the city proper.

I tried to find all the evangelical churches I could in the city, but I only discovered seven or eight that preached the gospel. I went to the university campus. I went into the inner city. I went to places where young people hung out. I went to the ethnic neighborhoods. I saw building after building, and home after home, person after person who did not know the Lord Jesus Christ, and it all seemed to be too much for me. I felt that there was hardly any hope. Humanly speaking, it seemed impossible.

I remember one night in particular. I knelt and began to pray in desperation to the Lord. In fact, I gave the Lord an opportunity to admit that he had made a mistake in inviting me to come to the city. But he didn't change his mind. Instead he began to call me to work alongside other Christians who were in the city. Together he wanted to use us to make an impact on that city. As I prayed, faith began to grow in my heart that God could make a difference.

I had been reading the book of Jonah, and I was struck by how weak Jonah was. He went the opposite direction when God called him to Nineveh. He was a proud prophet, a man who hated the Assyrians, the archenemies of Israel. Yet that was the man God used in Nineveh. He went and simply proclaimed the gospel, and God used his obedience to make a profound impact on that city. The whole city turned toward God in fasting and prayer. And I began to believe that it could happen again. If God could touch the wicked city of Nineveh, the capital of Assyria, then he could touch the city of Amsterdam.

I took a little piece of paper out, as I knelt in prayer, and I began to list all of the peoples that I had seen as I walked the streets—the university students, the drug addicts, the homosexuals. I listed all of the minority and ethnic groups I could find. There are one hundred fifteen languages spoken in the city of Amsterdam and forty-four major ethnic neighborhoods. As I listed the people groups, I began to ask the Lord to somehow start a ministry among every one of those peoples. I prayed that they would experience God's grace and God's hope in a way that would be understandable and meaningful to them.

Not a Christian City—Yet

That was fourteen years ago, and today I am thankful to tell you that God has begun to answer those prayers. When we first went to Amsterdam, there was no association of Christian groups or ministers. In fact, I invited some of the Christian leaders to meet on the little houseboat where we lived. It was so unusual in the nation of Holland at that time for evangelical ministers and leaders to meet together that the national news media sent out a television crew to film it.

We began to meet monthly. That group has met every month since that time. We call it The Evangelical Contact. There are now more than fifty churches and parachurch organizations that meet every month and have a wonderful spirit of unity. God has begun to touch the city of Amsterdam.

We were thrilled when Billy Graham came with the International Congress for Itinerant Evangelists in 1983 and again in 1986. Can you imagine ten thousand evangelists sitting in a conference for two weeks without preaching? Impossible. Every street corner had a black or a brown or a yellow face proclaiming the gospel. Every tram and train and bus had moving street meetings.

During the conference my wife was walking down the street and heard a man mumbling to himself. As she walked beside him, he was shaking his head and mumbling the word Jesus. "Oh, Jesus, Jesus, Jesus," he said. "Everywhere I go I can hear nothing but Jesus."

One young German tourist saw teams of young people with crosses. (Arthur Blessitt had been to town, so we had crosses everywhere.) Innocently she asked one of our workers, "I've gone to almost every major square in the city. I've been in bars and cafes and restaurants. Everywhere I've gone I've met Christians. Is this a Christian city?" It's not a Christian city—yet.

A Week of Ministry

In our organization, Youth With A Mission, there are over two hundred staff working full-time in the city. There are twenty-four full-time evangelistic and caring ministries. We have church planting teams, halfway houses, neighborhood Bible studies and a church renewal team. There are children's Bible clubs, bands, drama groups, a ministry to prostitutes and urban training programs.

I'd like to take you through a week so you can see what God has done. On Tuesday night there is a Bible study that is led by my former secretary. Laura was a missionary in South America for about sixteen years. She's sixty-nine years old. Four years ago she said to me, "I would like to start a Bible study for Spanish-speaking prostitutes." Thousands of them in the city have been brought in from Latin America. So she started with two or three people four years ago. Today she has Bible studies for seventy converted Spanish-speaking prostitutes on three nights of the week in three different cities. The result? I've lost my secretary. A few weeks ago she told me, "I can't serve you and keep going with the Bible studies. They are multiplying too much. You'll have to find another secretary."

Also on Tuesday night we have a work in the red-light district that is centered in what we call The Cleft. The Cleft is a little residence, a retreat, a hiding place for people in need who come to us. We also run a restaurant, where we serve Dutch pancakes. One Christmas, a Muslim man joined us for some free meals during the holidays. He had experienced the fellowship and the warmth. He went back to Germany where he lived and didn't quite understand how to contact us, so he wrote a letter and addressed it to The Cleft Pancake House Church.

Every Tuesday night, workers from The Cleft go on the streets of the red-light district and invite prostitutes, drug addicts and anybody who will come to a Bible study. They share the gospel, they give a free meal, and more than that they get involved in people's lives. For example, a few weeks ago there was a lady I'll call Paula who was standing out in front of The Cleft. She was invited in for a meal. After a lot of imploring she finally came. Paula had been a prostitute and a heroin addict for over twenty years. That night the grace of God finally broke into Paula's life. Weeping, she discovered that God loved her and forgave her.

Paula is now in a rehabilitation program. Every time I've seen her in the last few months, there has been a glow on her face. She can hardly enter into a Bible study or a Christian church service without weeping because of the joy that she has found in being forgiven by the Lord Jesus.

On Wednesday nights we have a Bible study that is for punks and other Amsterdam young people. About three years ago, a young man on our staff named David said he was concerned for the alienated youth of Amsterdam, especially the punkers. It is estimated that one out of every three seventeen-year-olds in Amsterdam is involved in homosexuality. Seventy per cent of the children born in the inner city are born to unwed mothers. Because of the surveys we have done, we estimate that in the nation of Holland eighty-five to ninety per cent of the young people are still interested in God, but they have turned their back on formal religion. It is a city with tremendous social problems and tremendous spiritual potential for the young.

For eighteen months David and his team of workers went out night after night into the nightclubs and the cafes of the city. They did not see one person respond to the gospel.

Then about a year and a half ago, they started a Bible study. Young people began to come. David is very contemporary (and very appropriate to Amsterdam) in the way he communicates. He started a punk band called No Longer Music. Some would debate whether it's a band or not. They do make noise. Joyful noise. It's a very colorful Bible study they have now. It's been a breakthrough. About one hundred-fifty punks have come to know the Lord Jesus along with many other Amsterdam young people.

Eddie, one of the young people who became a Christian, was kicked out of his home when he was eight years old. His father told him he never wanted to see Eddie again. That was eleven years ago. A year ago, Eddie heard about what the press had begun to call the Chrunk movement—the Christian punks. (Leave it to the press to come up with a name like that.) As a result he came to David's Bible study. When Eddie saw young people like himself who were excited about God, who were dealing with the issues that he was facing, he considered Christianity.

Eddie found Jesus Christ a few weeks later, and then a national television team came and interviewed him. He gave his testimony. His father saw Eddie on television for the first time in ten years. The next day Eddie got a telephone call. The day after that they had lunch together, and they were reconciled together as father and son after ten years of alienation.

Also on Wednesday nights, a Christian family in another part of the city leads a new congregation. They moved into a neighborhood of about twenty-five thousand people where there was no active church and began a Bible study. The husband began going door-to-door while still working in business full time. Later he brought in teams of people to help him. Now there is a new church in that neighborhood. On Thursday nights we have a Bible study for Iranians. There are many refugees from Iran all over Europe. There's a young man, a German, who leads our work with Muslims. On Friday nights he leads a Bible study for Moroccans. I asked Harry why he didn't have the Bible study on the same night since the Iranians and Moroccans were both Muslims. He reminded me that there was a war going on in the Middle East. He said, "My goal is to get both groups converted and then we'll bring them together."

On Saturday, believe it or not, we have a Bible study for normal people. We have a young lady who coordinates our follow-up in Amsterdam, and she came to me very excited in the spring of this year. "Floyd, you won't believe this! We've had a great breakthrough. Yesterday in the outreach, two normal Dutch girls got saved."

One of the young men who became a Christian in our work when we first moved to Amsterdam fourteen years ago was John Goodfellow, a thief from the streets of Nottingham, England. After going back to Nottingham to make restitution for some of the crimes he committed, he rejoined us. He'd seen a street preacher in Nottingham, and he wanted to preach on the streets of Amsterdam.

At that time we emphasized friendship evangelism. I had experienced street meetings, but I didn't like them. I had seen people standing on street corners in America preaching about hell and yelling at people. I had a negative impression of what street meetings were like. So when John asked about this, I said, "No way!" And a few weeks later, he came and asked me again. And I said, "No, we're into friendship evangelism. We want to care for people. We love people. We don't want to yell at them."

Over a six-month period, he came back to me about every two or three weeks. He wouldn't give up. One night, I was walking down the hallway in the building where we were living, and I heard a voice. Listening more closely, I realized someone was praying. It was John, weeping and crying as he interceded with God. Then I heard him praying for me, "Oh, God, please change his mind. Lord, touch his heart. Please, Lord, let him give me permission to go on the streets and preach the gospel."

So the next day I said to John that he could go—on two conditions."John, please don't yell at people, and please don't talk about hell." He was so excited he would have done anything. John with some others went out on the streets of Amsterdam to the main square, and I stood in the back of the crowd and watched. They used some folk dancing to attract a crowd. Dutch people, especially the Amsterdamers as we call them, love something that has joy, that has humor in it.

John told the people about the joy the Lord had brought into his heart as somebody who had found Jesus on the streets of Amsterdam. He shared how he had become a thief, running from the law, running from problems. But he had found the joy of his salvation in Jesus. I was amazed as I stood watching at how open people were to a loving, joyful presentation of the good news of the gospel. We outjoyed the joy that they had known in the world. Many people came to those meetings that we began to conduct on the streets.

I began to read about the early days of the Salvation Army, and I read a book called *The General Next to God.* The Salvation Army was too stubborn to give up. When they went into a city, if they couldn't penetrate it, they tried something else. They would keep trying different approaches, with different people groups until finally they would break through.

I read about one young lady, an officer in the Salvation Army, who was having a hard time in one city. So she decided to have a funeral. She got a coffin, got a young officer to be the dead person and put him in the coffin. They walked down the street and finally stopped and leaned the coffin against the building. When the crowd they gathered was big enough, this young man jumped out and began to preach on "The Wages of Sin is Death."

So I told John about this, and a few days later heard some hammering in our basement. I went downstairs and discovered John building a seven-foot black coffin. Since that time we've had many funeral services in Amsterdam.

John now heads a ministry in Amsterdam we call the Go Teams. This last summer, between May and August, John had teams in nineteen different countries. A team in Bombay helped plant five churches in three months working with missionaries there. Another team was in North Africa worked with a small, struggling church of about sixty believers. It was doubled in two and a half weeks as seventy people found faith in Jesus Christ. They're still preaching the gospel.

The Dark Continent
I love the city of Amsterdam. I celebrate the Lord Jesus in that city. I believe that God longs for and looks for those who will go to the

cities of our world. Amsterdam is a city that is surrounded within a mile radius by one hundred-fifty million people. Europe is a continent of great need. It is a spiritual wasteland.

Though there is great revival in China, though the church is growing three times as fast as the population in Latin America, though there are some days in Africa that up to twenty thousand people a day become Christians, in Europe we have not experienced the touch yet of God's Spirit in great renewal. We have not seen the church turned around. There are five hundred-fifty million people living in Western Europe. About seventy per cent of them live in cities, and of that seventy per cent, it is estimated that less than two per cent go to church on Sundays.

I present to you Europe as a mission field.

I remind you of cities like Amsterdam and Paris and London which desperately need the gospel of Jesus Christ. Amsterdam has more than four hundred financial institutions. It's one of the seven or eight most influential financial cities in the world. It is a city that waits to hear the good news of Jesus Christ.

I discovered in reading the book of Jonah that God uses ordinary people to do extraordinary things. If we will simply follow the example of our Lord Jesus, if we will give up our rights, if we will be willing to give up our reputation, if we will come as servants to stand beside people, not over them but beside them, to love them and share joyfully and lovingly and patiently the good news that we have discovered, many people will respond.

Floyd McClung, Jr., is executive director of international operations and director of urban missions for Youth With A Mission, a worldwide ministry training young adults in missions.

8
The City and Unreached Peoples

Harvie M. Conn

WHAT IS A CITY? FOR A NORTH AMERICAN WHITE, A CITY IS A MELTING POT. FOR a suburbanite it's a ghetto. For my next-door neighbor in inner-city Philadelphia, a city is "one large collection of nothings."

Now all these definitions are wrong, and they're all wrong for the same reason. Yuppie, suburbanite or black, most people can't see anything in the city except mathematical urban units of one. They're often like the pastor I met once in our ministry in Korea. At a moment of truth he confided in me, "I have a very hard time telling all you Americans apart. You look so alike." I think that's how we all see cities. They all look so alike—sort of an urbanized Charles Bronson death wish.

A rose is a rose is a rose. And a city is a city is a city—a monoclass stereotype where everything becomes the least pleasant denominator. And when you see nothing else, you resort again to that Norman Rockwell world view, the melting-pot myth where everything looks so nice and everyone is equal—of course some are more equal than others. In this scheme we're all in this together, and there's plenty of room for those that must sit in the back of the bus. We're all one big happy family. Tell that to the single parent on welfare in Newark, New Jersey. Ethnic differences, poor and rich neighborhoods, Yuppies, blue collar workers, physicians, roofers—they all slowly evaporate into this new homogeneity that is usually identified only as urban.

Now, what does all this have to do with world missions? You can't reach what you can't see.

Take a look, for example, at Lima, Peru. If you took your first look in 1984, you would find a city somewhere between four and a half and six million people, which, by the way, account for one-third of the total population of Peru. In 1982 people were moving into the capital city of Lima at a rate of 230 people per day. Today it is several times that figure, but if that is all you notice about Lima, your picture is still too general. You still haven't seen what you need to see to minister effectively there.

Lima is full of migrants, migrants from the provinces and the remotest Andean villages. And as you look closely, you will notice that they don't lose their identity as soon as they get off the bus. You won't see them with their knees shaking, looking around ready to have a mental breakdown because suddenly they've made it to the big city. Instead they come to the city and form social clubs, organized around their home locality. These regional clubs give them a place to gather, to feel at home in their new surroundings, a buffer zone that cushions the impact of the new urban world that they are part of. In 1957 there were 200 such associations in Lima. By 1984 there were more than 6,000. Now don't tell these people that Lima is a melting pot. Lima is a salad bowl. In fact, it may be 6,000 salad bowls awaiting the gospel's salad dressing.

Look again. Here's another Lima—the Lima you see on the street, an army of street venders, 200,000 to 300,000 strong. Up to 70% of the urban labor force in Lima make up this nonformal business world.

Look again and see Lima's 10,000 abandoned children. They shine shoes, wash cars, change tires and go begging during the day. At night they sleep in parks or on the sidewalk. They are a part of the fifty per cent of Lima's population that is under 22 years of age.

When you look at Lima like this, what do you see? You see magnetic centers that are sucking or pulling people into their fields. These magnetic fields are people groups. And they pull in different ways. Sometimes the pull is language or ethnicity. For example, 30% of the 18,000,000 Peruvians speak only Quechua. Yet there are only two

Quechua-language evangelical congregations in all of Lima.

Sometimes the bonding that holds people together is geography, social space, a commonly shared residential territory. Migrants, for example, in Lima pour into something called the *pueblos jóvenes,* a euphemism meaning "young towns" to the government, but "slums" to the city. Three of every ten Limeños live in one of these young towns. The children who fill them live on a cup of tea and a couple of bread rolls a day. And an inflation rate of 125% keeps them there.

Sometimes the bonding that brings people together into a group is nongeographic social space. The street vendors and abandoned children represent such groups. Sometimes vocations bring non-neighbors together. Sometimes its common interests.

For seven years in Korea I did evangelistic work in brothels, sharing Christ with the country's prostitute population of over 50,000. They too represent a people group. A new and massive people group has emerged in just the last decade. It crosses ethnic, linguistic and even social barriers. I speak of those suffering from AIDS.

Some months ago I was visiting the midwest, and a friend invited me to go to a midnight prayer meeting. We went into this row house and up a set of rickety stairs and opened the door. There was this long table and about twelve people sitting around it, all with Bibles in front of them with beer cans strewn all over the smoke-filled room.

The Bible study leader was at the end, smoking this long, black cigar—and she really enjoyed it. At the other end of the table was this guy, built like Sylvester Stallone, wearing a black T-shirt with a white skull on it. On one arm was a big tattoo, a heart with the word *mother* on it and a big dagger through it.

So we sat down for a two-hour Bible study. Having been teaching at a typical white suburban theological seminary where everything's safe, I had my doubts when things started, but when we were done, I had no doubts about what was going on. These were people who really loved the Lord, most of them brand new believers. The gentleman at the end of the table with the tattoo had been responsible for leading almost everyone there to Christ.

These were bikers. They wouldn't feel much at home in our community or in most of our churches. Two or three of the members of the Bible study were former members of Hell's Angels. A member of the Christian Biker's Association, the fellow who started the Bible study spends six months of the year with his wife on the road, and his whole ministry is spent trying to reach bikers for Jesus. "Most outsiders," he told me, "are turned off by the beer and cigars. You ought to have seen what they were smoking and drinking a few months ago. Some Christians start at 1; other, at -3."

I had found another unreached people group, one I didn't have to travel overseas to find. And I had also been reminded that sanctification follows justification, not vice versa.

What does this all mean for world evangelization? It means we need to realize that cities are not single, homogeneous little packages—Limas, Lisbons and Los Angeleses. They are conglomerates of thousands of different people groups. There are TV-movie entertainers in Seoul, soccer teams playing in São Paulo, Brazil; there are truck drivers spending 12-15 hours on the road between Osaka and Toyko. There are the cosmopolitans of Singapore, who communicate only in English, their class-consciousness high, their ethnic-consciousness low.

Last summer, as a classroom experiment, I sent three teams of missionaries to Times Square in New York. Their assignment: to survey the same area of about six city blocks in the course of an evening and to come back the next day with a list of fifteen unreached peoples.

The next morning we all gathered to present our lists. They included over fifty people groups with an overlap of only three or four. In the same area we came across only three Christian groups and churches, and only one of those, we found out, was working with the people in that area. We also found that the bars in the area were much more aware of people groups than the church. There were gay bars, singles bars, bars for the theater crowd and bars for newspaper people. Remember the opening line of the Cheers theme song, ". . . where everybody knows your name"?

We had begun to see the unreached people of the city, visible to God, but too often invisible to us. On our list we put prostitutes, sidewalk vendors, tourists, police, gays, theater people, teenage runaways, bag ladies, the homeless, store owners. We found all sorts of gospel targets and no sharpshooters. And we were also discovering that if you aim at everything, you will hit nothing.

Urban People Groups from the New Testament

Look with me at still another city with its people groups. We'll pick one with heavy population density, perhaps 200 people per acre, the equivalent of the industrial slums of Chicago or Philadelphia. This city has been devastated by war, and it has been rebuilt and gentrified by its Yuppie population.

It has become a thriving commercial center and capital of its province. Its reputation is built on a combination of religion and sex—all without benefit of television or industrial-strength mascara. It's name has become a proverb for the good life, for a free-wheeling lifestyle. We're talking, of course, about the city of Corinth in the days of the apostle Paul.

The Lord had told the apostle Paul on his first visit to Corinth not to be afraid. "You don't have to hide in the suburbs, man. Don't forget what I did for Moses in Egypt. There are a lot of good folks in the city." That's my rough paraphrase of Acts 18:10.

Now when you read Romans, probably written from Corinth, and Paul's two letters written to the Christians in Corinth, you can see how God kept his promise. High and low, rich and poor, Jew and Greek—all the social, political and ethnic networks are there, and the gospel is touching them all.

Erastus—you find his name in the last chapter of Romans—either the director of the public works department (NIV) or the city treasurer (RSV) is there in Corinth. The aristocracy is being touched as well as the influential and the wealthy. First Corinthians 1 mentions Crispus. He came to Christ during Paul's first visit. Acts 18:18 calls him a ruler of the synagogue. That was a leader of the Jewish worship service, someone who assumed responsibility for the synagogue building. It also meant a man with money, social influence, far beyond the boundaries of the Jewish community itself.[1] I wonder if that isn't why in Acts 18:8 we read of the great impact of Crispus's conversion on the city. "Many of the Corinthians who heard him believed and were baptized."

He had a baptismal partner named Gaius. Romans 16:23 informs us that he was "host of the whole church" at Corinth, and that certainly means that he had a house big enough to put up Paul and to accommodate all the various Christian groups in Corinth that met together. He too was a fellow with some wealth and property.

At the other end of the social scale were the slaves, and the Corinthian Christian community included them as well. In fact, the numerical strength of the Corinthian church probably heavily leaned toward the have-nots of society. That's how God builds his church. With the wise and the powerful and the have-nots, all together doing the work of Jesus Christ.

In 1 Corinthians 1:26-28 Paul draws some gospel lessons against the background of these social realities. He paints a sociological picture of the church. There are "the wise," the educated classes; there are "the influential"; there are those of "noble birth." But there are "not many" of these in the church, though there are some.

By contrast, there are "the lower born," "the despised," "the things that are not." Primarily, among these people groups, "the refuse of the world, the offscouring of all things" (1 Cor 4:10-13 RSV), the church grows. And, says Paul in his best theological voice, that is the usual way God does things.

Is it easy to build an urban church out of such diverse groups? Not if Paul's experience is typical. First Corinthians 1 gives you a good sample of the problems.

Ethnic differences pick away at the gospel. Greeks look for wisdom; Jews look for power. What is needed is a new vision of Christ crucified, "the power of God and the wisdom of God" (1 Cor 1:24). Social differences create conceit. Wealthy and influential Christians presumably were looking down their "noble born" noses at the "have not" Christians. The answer, says Paul, is God's weird peculiarities of grace in election, the foolish things of this world chosen to shame the wise (1 Cor 1:27-28).

Biblical Guidelines for Reaching the Unreached in the City
What do we learn when wey read and hear all of this? At least three things, three messages from Paul's picture of Corinth to Urbana 87. Pull them out of your mailbag.

1. The cutting edge of the church in the city is evangelism. The cities of Paul's day were crowded with voluntary associations and private clubs. Mainly they existed for the purpose of getting together, especially for people of like interests and occupations. They had regular meetings, their odd-ball Shriner-like initiation rites and special meals.[2]

The Christian church looked a lot like one of these special clubs, I suspect. That's how they survived at first in the city. They had their regular meetings, they had their initiation rites, they looked a little kooky, they had their special meals, but they were a different kind of club. They were the only club that existed for the sake of its non-members. Always before our eyes, says Paul in his letters, must be those on the outside.

Artisans, says Paul, are to lead a quiet life, to mind their own business and to work with their hands (1 Thess 4:11). Why? That their "daily life may win the respect of outsiders" (1 Thess 4:12). Likewise, the Corinthian Christians must put no stumbling block before Jews and Greeks. The exercise of the gift of tongues in public assembly is to be restrained if visiting unbelievers get the wrong idea and think we Christians are insane. Any practices judged as disgraceful by the Gentiles must be curtailed (1 Cor 11:4-6). Colossians 4:5 sums it up: "Behave wisely toward the outsiders, and cash in your opportunities."

Evelyn Quema, a short, stout, single Filipina, is barely noticeable in a crowd of women her age. At the age of 22 she gave up her desire to be a lawyer or a doctor and moved to the city of Baguio. She arrived on a Thursday with six dollars and no place to live. By Sunday she had conducted a church service for thirty and saw four conversions. Three years later she had planted four churches and started eleven outstations, one of them five hours away by bus. She had seen 300 solid conversions to Christ and several hundred more professions that she had not been able to follow up. Miriam Adeney, who tells this story, adds, "There are hundreds of Christian women like Evelyn in Southeast Asia."

2. The cutting edge of the church in the city is evangelism to all unreached peoples. Paul's churches saw that. Membership went from slave owner to slave (Eph 6:5-9; Col 3:22—4:1), from the household of Caesar to manual laborers, skilled or unskilled (Phil 3:22; 2 Thess 3:6-13). We find wealthy artisans and traders like Lydia with high incomes but low occupational prestige. We find poor Christians in Jerusalem, recipients of financial support from poor Christians in Corinth and Macedonia (1 Cor 16:1-4).

This is one of the reasons that the poor are so prominent in the New Testament. Not because they have special privileges in heaven or because they can get in on the basis of an empty savings account. But because God really does love every economic and social class, and because the wealthy, and sadly enough even wealthy Christians, are often in danger of forgetting them. Marginalized minorities and powerful majorities—the Lord has room for all of them in his church.

There are about 10,000 Muslims in my city, Philadelphia. About 80% of them are American Blacks. Too many of them are like my former next-door neighbor. They grew up in Christian homes, worshiped in Christian churches and finally turned to Islam. Why? My neighbor put it to me this way, "The most segregated hour of the week in America is Sunday morning at 11:00 A.M. I dig Jesus. I just don't like his church." An unreached people have become an invisible people.

The picture is the same around the world. The church in too many cities listen to too many sermons on success rather than suffering, while many feel left out in the ecclesiastical cold.

The industrial workers of Taiwan—three million of them—complain "that the message of local churches is irrelevant to their daily life and most programs are geared toward the needs of the intellectuals or the middle class."[3] Over 40% of Singapore's workforce is blue collar, production-industry workers. Yet only 4% of them are Christians.

At the bottom of society's value scale, and often the church's, are the poor, the squatters, the new urban migrants. Forty-six per cent of Mexico City's population, 67% of Calcutta's, 60% of Kinshasa's, live in slums. And the gap between them and the church now grows into a gulf.

Yet they hear the word gladly. In the hall here at Urbana a missionary recounted to me how he had targeted Japanese businessmen for Christ, inviting them to play golf with him. Their response to this "golf evangelism" was largely negative, but one of the caddies listened as they walked and talked. He in turn talked to other caddies, many of whom came to Christ through his witness.. This missionary was wise enough to see what the Holy Spirit was doing and shifted his attention to a people group he had never seen before—Japanese golf caddies.

How do you tell which unreached people group in the city to focus on when there are so many? You watch for the footprints of the Lord and follow that trail.

Viv Grigg, a New Zealander, has made the same discovery about Jesus, "a companion to the poor." In 1979 he moved into Tatalon, a squatter community of 14,500 people, jammed into six city blocks in Manila. Now he pleads for the Lord's people to join him in creating Christian communities in the slums and shanty towns of the world. A new mission board has come out of his kingdom perspective called Servants among the Poor. An old vision has been renewed: mobile men and women, freed for pioneering, prophetic, evangelistic church planting among the poor. How does he put it? "The greatest mission surge in history has entirely missed the greatest migration in history, the migration of Third World peasants to great mega-cities."[4]

3. The cutting edge of the church in the city is lordship evangel-

ism—*Jesus proclaimed by word and deed, Jesus our justification and our justice.*

A biblical call to repentance and faith in Christ does not call us away from the city; it calls us to live under the lordship of Jesus Christ in every area of the city. Personal commitment to Jesus is foundational. But on that foundation we erect a model home, living out the full implications of the gospel for urban Christians.

Isn't that how Paul saw it as he wrote to Corinth? I have heard people say that Paul never dealt with social, political or economic issues. But that doesn't square with the list of pastoral questions he tries to answer in 1 Corinthians—ethnocentrism, the social gap between rich and poor, lawsuits, sex and prostitutes, slavery, homosexuality, women's liberation.

Cities like Corinth or Colomb don't let you get away with dividing your Christian life into safety zones—one zone labeled faith, another the world. Ask Malcolm X. American racism turned him from talkative Christianity to what he saw as real brotherhood in Islam. Ask the Black Christians of Soweto. A plea for peace without justice can turn good news into cheap grace. "I was sick and you did not look after me; I was under the ban and you never visited me." Ask the Blacks and Latinos who come to Urbana. Ask them why you have to search so hard to find their brothers and sisters on the mission field abroad or on this platform at Urbana or on the mission boards represented at the armory. It's hard to hear "Go into all the world" when the same voices don't also say, "Come into all our neighborhoods."

Paul saw a social revolution brewing in the things we now identify as "church matters." A simple table meal to remember the Lord's death shatters social hierarchies long held sacred. At Corinth the wealthy apparently were making the Lord's Supper into a "private dinner party" (1 Cor 11:21). And when the meal was over, the haves were drunk and the have-nots were hungry. Paul calls for a new kind of urban social order to be built from the table and the sacrifice that had prepared it (1 Cor 10:16-17; 11:18-19). Wealth in the body of Christ becomes an opportunity to serve, prestige a call to humility.

None of this is easy in the city. Political and social networks fit together too tightly. You may find yourself one day a missionary pastor in a Central American country, the members of your congregation united in their commitment to Christ but divided in their political allegiances. Late one evening a knock may come to your door. There in front of you stands a member of your congregation, a brother in Christ with strong antigovernment sympathies. There is a bullet in his arm; blood drips down his coat. "Pastor," he asks, "can I stay the night with you?" Suddenly your Christian response to a brother becomes a political decision.

More than ten years ago I was on a mountain in Korea. I was up there for three days of evangelistic meetings at an isolated village with no electricity. I was talking that night on the love of Christ and how Christians love one another, and at the end asked if there were any questions. An old man raised his hand and said "I have a question, sir," he said. "If Christians are supposed to love one another, how do you explain what happened in Birmingham?"

There we were on the top of the mountain in the middle of nowhere and this old farmer with a horsehair hat asked me about Birmingham. In the barbershop in the village that day, they got a newspaper, the only newspaper this village ever got. There it was spread out in front of the barbershop and all the villagers were reading it. On the front page was a picture of Bull Conner letting the dogs loose on the Black Christians praying in Birmingham, Alabama. Suddenly I discovered that the questions of racism and reaching unreached peoples are not two separate questions.

In 1890 the Southern Presbyterian Church sent to the Congo a man who had learned these things. William Henry Shepherd spent twenty years in Africa. Respected by the Africans, he was called "Shoppit Monine, the Great Sheppard." Working among the Bokuba people, he showed a cultural respect and sensitivity for things African seldom seen among missionaries of his day. He knew how large this simple gospel was.

The Jesus that he preached was revolutionary in African society. For example, he resisted the custom of killing a slave to accompany a recently deceased master. He protested against the practice of trial by poison. When the Belgian government imposed a heavy food tax on the people, he protested. The tax forced the Africans to work for Europeans to pay it, a subtle form of colonialism. In addition, the government used soldiers who were cannibals to collect the tax. Shepherd discovered that the tax-collecting efforts were a cover for slave raids and for cannibalism. His protests brought the entire issue to the attention of King Leopold of Belgium. Strained relations with the government and with his mission finally brought him back to the States in retirement in 1910.

Sheppard had gone to Africa when the White Churches had almost no interest in Africa for Christ. Sheppard was Black, one of the 113 American Blacks who served in Africa from 1877 to 1900.

Who can tell how many Bakubans heard the word of Christ and believed because they saw Sheppard standing for the oppressed and the sinned against. How many there saw Sheppard himself as one of those sinned against? Could it have been that which brought them to Jesus Christ and to the cross?

What deed done for Christ will yet stir the hearts of the urban world's unreached peoples to hear the word spoken by Christ? And who will speak it and who will go do it?

Harvie M. Conn, former missionary in Korea, is professor of missions and director of the urban missions program at Westminster Theological Seminary in Philadelphia.

Notes

[1] Gerd Theissen, *The Social Setting of Pauline Christianity* (Philadelphia: Fortress, 1982), pp.74–75.

[2] Wayne Meeks, *The Moral World of the First Christians* (Philadelphia: Westminster, 1986), pp.113–14.

[3] Quoted in Harvie M. Conn, *A Clarified Vision for Urban Mission* (Grand Rapids: Zondervan, 1987), p. 162.

[4] Viv Grigg, "Sorry! The Frontier Moved," *Urban Mission* 4, no. 4 (March 1987), p. 13.

9
Panel
on Urban
Mission

Elward Ellis, Ray Bakke, Floyd McClung,
Harvie Conn

ELLIS: WE'VE BEEN TALKING ABOUT THE CITIES OF THE WORLD, AND I WAS trying to put myself in the position of some of you to anticipate what questions you might have. Floyd, you told us you moved into the red-light district, places where there are brothels and prostitutes and X-rated parlors, and you also told us that you moved your two children and your wife there. Let's suppose I'm at the University of Illinois studying and trying to take a serious look at God's call for my life, but I'm apprehensive about going into a place where so much sin and wickedness, titillation and tantalization, and all those other *ations* are going on. What I want to know is how I can responsibly care for my children in an environment like that?

McClung: I think that when Sally and I weighed and evaluated the pressures there would be on our family, including the violence and the vandalism, we came to see that there are subtle forms of evil as well as overt forms of evil. I feel that there are just as many dangers living in a suburban area as there are in the city. We can easily see the visible forms of immorality, but we don't often see the more subtle kinds of sin like creeping materialism, or compromising comfort, or the value system that says that security is found in a three-bedroom, two-bathroom, two-car garage house.

There are pressures on children in suburban schools that can compromise their Christianity perhaps even more easily than the more overt forms of what we call sin. I think it's important also, when we talk about danger, that we recognize that the danger is perceived by people that live outside that area. The people inside those areas don't think there is danger there. They feel very much at home there.

We've learned not to go walking at certain times of the day and in certain places. It's easy to avoid that kind of evil. But what do you do to avoid the kinds of sins, the kinds of pressures and temptations, in the suburbs?

And I want to say to you who are raising families, "Please don't flee. Please don't base your values on those that have been passed on to you with only a very superficial look at what is really best for your family. Maybe the very best thing you could do for your family is to raise them in a neighborhood where they would not be escaping the realities of our world. Living in a white suburban neighborhood could cause us to escape from what is happening in 90% of our world, and I don't know if that's really best for our children.

Bakke: Corean and I raised three sons that have combined over thirty years of schooling in the Chicago inner-city school system. And while they may be behind in math and science and English, I think they're two to ten years ahead of national norms in social skills. And when my kid went against my adopted Black kid for homecoming king and the white kid won in an inner-city school where he was a minority kid, I said, "How did you win?" And he said, "I got the Arab, Black and Chinese vote!"

It's very obvious that there are many benefits to being in an inner-city school. And let's be honest, missionaries have often buried some of their children on the foreign field. The Lord calls us to risk, and the power of being in the city with your children is incredible. They know you didn't come there to cause trouble, they know you're not a detective, and they will accept you. And your children give you entrée. Isaiah 40:11 makes it very clear: "[the Lord] gently leads those that have young." And that applies to crossing guards, day-care directors, school-bus drivers and those of you who take your children to the city.

Ellis: Thank you. I was born and raised in the inner-city central ward of Newark, New Jersey, and have been the victim of too many in-migrations of too many starry-eyed idealistic suburban people who have come to save me over and over again. How do we avoid un-leashing on the cities of the world people with a messiah complex?

Conn: I think the last thing our neighborhood needs is a whole bunch of you folks. You folks come into our area, and the real estate folks will hike up the prices on the houses, the tax base will go up, and then folks like us can move out and look for another slum. This whole question of gentrification is an important one.

The real issue, though, is your commitments. Don't come into the city if it just means a place that is next to the local museums. Don't come into the city unless you are prepared to commit yourself to the city as your mission field. That means a commitment that will entail a great many things. It should entail, it seems to me, ministry in the churches that exist in the city. You're going to have to learn to be crosscultural.

You whites in this audience, if you come to the city, put yourself under the discipleship of a Black church or Hispanic church to learn what it really means to be a servant of Jesus in the city. If you can't do that, it raises some questions of your coming. You can't be a missionary in Korea if you go there and then insist all the Koreans there learn English. You work with the church there.

It means also, you must be involved in the cities. You've got to get involved with the networks that are there, the things Ray talks about in his great little book *The Urban Christian.* You've got to become part of God's mobile force in the city. You want the church and you want your home to be a demonstration model. In the city "occupying until he comes" doesn't mean that you board up your house and fill it with ten years of back issues of HIS magazine until the Lord comes to restore. No, you break out and you say, How can I function as a Christian in the city. We've heard great things about how Floyd does it in Amsterdam. I don't know why those kinds of things can't work anywhere. That's lordship evangelism. Don't come unless you're equipped to do that.

Ellis: There is a theme running through these talks that shows us the need of people groups in the city, and it really plucks our heartstrings. We are being motivated to give of ourselves to the Lord that he might give of himself to the people in need. How do Christians benefit personally from their contact with people whose needs they seek to meet?

Bakke: There's no way you can know enough to enter a city. The only way is to come to learn. When you approach people and allow them to teach you, you will learn an incredible amount. One of the best examples of that is a colleague of mine, Claude Marie Barbour, who after being a missionary in South Africa, beaten, brutalized and terrorized, went into the Black community of Chicago to be ministered unto. A group of people surrounded her and started caring for her, and out of that came a shalom-based community movement that is unbelievable.

Team-teaching with Claude Marie, I've learned that the poor and nonschooled—in the sense of formal training—are often quadrilingual. They have often worked through multicultural experience. They come with experience that is not in the textbooks, and if you come to listen to the stories, you'll have a continuing education experience for the rest of your life.

McClung: I believe the greatest qualifier for anyone who wants to serve others is humility. The example of the Lord Jesus is that he gave up his reputation, he left his home, he gave up all that he had in his beautiful home, and he came to earth and became a servant. He washed people's feet, he listened to them, he cared for them, he touched them, he went to their homes, and if we will approach people as servants, to learn, if we will come and be a friend and listen and take time to be with people, whether it's short term or long term, we can have a significant ministry whether for an hour or for the rest of our lives. The important thing is how we approach people. If we come as the great savior to save them, if we diagnose their problems and impose on them our solutions, that smacks of a spirit that people are rejecting in our world of being manipulated, of being used and exploited. But if we come as servants, if we come to learn from them and hear them and weep with them and then to share what God has done for us, then they will listen to us.

Ellis: Our brother Ajith Fernando has spoken to us about the environment of people affecting their ability to be righteous. Does the Christian have a responsibility, and if so, how, to evangelize and disciple and bring justice to bear in the lives of the movers and shakers—the people who wield power in the business and economic community and the government?

Conn: I think the answer is yes. The big question is, How are we going to do that? In a setting like the U.S. and Canada, where there is a free and open type of government, Christians have high, easy access, and sadly enough, they don't make use of it. They can run for office, and they can be elected.

Some of you, however, are going to go into Muslim states. You won't have that privilege. By Muslim law you will be closed in a ghetto community. You won't have that access. Your problem then will be how to teach new believers and disciple them regarding how they can function in that setting. Some of you like me will go to work in a right-wing dictatorship or totalitarian government, and you may find that the pressures are equally strong on any side. You will also find that the government will be happy if all you do is "preach Christ." But never give attention to Romans 13.

In those kinds of settings, I think the Bible starts coming alive when it talks about suffering. And you begin to wrestle with how difficult it is to function in cities and to speak to cities even as a Christian because of the complexity of it all, and you don't know how to get a handle on it.

Suppose you're a missionary in Central America, and you're pastoring a church in Nicaragua, like someone I know. Among the members of your church are some supporters of the government as well as some contras. Suppose that one night you hear the gate of your house at the front street open around midnight, and you hear a knock at your front door. Lights are going on all down the street. People are seeing what's happening. In front of you is a member of your congregation, and he has a bullet in his arm. He's been bleeding from the gate to your front door. You don't want to get involved in politics. You're a missionary. You're just a guest in the country. And then the man says to you, "Pastor, can I come in for the night?"

No matter which way you turn, you've just made a political decision. It's totally taken out of your hands by the setting and the situation. I don't know the answers to those kinds of questions sometimes. But I think it just adds to the pain and the struggle that we're all going to have because we have to face those situations in the world of which we're a part. And even as we do that, our heart aches and we're thinking these things have to change. You get in there by God's grace and you do what you can. But sometimes it's awfully tough.

The woman that I've talked about, Miss Kim we call her, did evangelistic work. When she was working with Communist students in Korea, she asked them once, so she could better understand Marxism, what books she should read. They told her she should read Karl Marx's *Das Kapital.*

So she went to the library of the largest university in Seoul, which she never should have done, and she asked for a copy of the book. And they told her that it was specially reserved and that she should come back tomorrow. That night the Korean CIA took her from her home, placed her in a political prison. Two years later I went to see her in prison. She died in that prison two years after that. She never went to trial. Her grave is outside the back gate of this particular prison. Her major crime was taking a book out of the library.

There are a lot of Christians in many parts of the world who are facing those kinds of trials and struggles. Sometimes all you can do is cry, and sometimes all you can do is bleed with them.

Bakke: Even though as a missionary you are a guest in a country and can't take all the up-front risk, you must not water down the gospel. Preach the themes of justice and God's love and care for the poor. That's a subversive message that ultimately, as Paul knew, will work its way up to the palace. It will percolate up from the bottom. The early church wrestled with the issue of government from the optimism of Romans 13 and the early Pauline mission to the pessimism of Revelation 13—the same government they realized wasn't going to yield. And I think that within that thirty-year span in the New Testament we discover that the early church found at some points they could work with governments and other points they had to actively resist them.

Ellis: One last question—maybe two. What is the role, as you experts see it, of women in the mission of Christ in the city?

McClung: To quote William Booth, I believe some of God's best men are women. I personally believe that there's nothing a man can do that a woman can't do or do better. The Scripture makes it very clear that there is equality in who we are in Christ. There are different ministries, there are different giftings, and I believe we all, male or female, can have any of the ministries that are described in Scripture.

There are times when it's better for women to do things than for men to do them. In our neighborhood, it is much wiser for women to work with the prostitutes. As soon as a man goes to a prostitute, there's a question mark in her mind about why he is there. So we never allow men to go two by two. It's better for women to go two by two, or if a man goes, for him to go with a woman.

I've seen woman church planters. I've seen women working in Muslim countries where the mission executives said they couldn't do it. Yet I know of a Muslim country where two women opened a ministry. The government said, "If you keep going and preaching the gospel the way you are, we'll close you down." The women said "Fine, close us down, but we won't stop." They were fearless and bold. Those women are reaching more Saudi Arabians and more Muslims than any other Muslim ministry in the world today.

Ellis: One last question. One of the most difficult challenges we face in preaching the gospel in the Black community in the U.S. is the reputation of White and Black Christians in the church. One of the most difficult challenges is to make Jesus make sense when our relationships don't make sense. Can you give us some challenge or encouragement in the role of our relationships across racial barriers in the U.S. to mission strategy?

McClung: You know I've had a painful awareness during this conference that there hasn't been a Black, Hispanic, Campuchean or Vietnamese sitting on the platform or speaking, and we're talking about urban missions. I feel it's a real privilege to be here. And I know that some of you who are Black or Hispanic probably find it pretty painful that you don't have somebody representing you, and I want to say personally that I am aware of that and I wrestle with that. I don't take that for granted. I don't blame you if you have a certain amount of mistrust for White-led agencies that don't fellowship with you, that don't embrace you, that don't seek you out, but do come to you and say, "Come and help us reach Black people in Africa."

We need to recognize this as Whites, that if we're not in meaningful, legitimate, honest relationships here, then all of a sudden to say, "Let's go over there and reach those Black people" raises a giant question mark on our integrity. We Whites have to recognize that if we're not in legitimate and honest relationships in our own cities here, then there's a good chance that we'll be very paternalistic somewhere else, and we'll come looking down on people.

I personally have to wrestle with a lot of prejudices in my heart and deal with those kinds of issues. I would call on us to bring integrity to our mission through honest relationships where we grapple with issues and we talk openly and honestly with brothers and sisters of different races. Then we go in partnership. That will allow us to go in genuine partnership to people on other continents who are of different races. I work in Amsterdam as a partner with people who are working there. I work in Nigeria with people who are partners there.

Ellis: I've got a partner on the platform who wants us to sit down. I want to make a quick book plug in the tradition of this convention. Some of you don't know anything about the African American history of missions. Most African Americans don't. Two books you might want to seek out: *Black Americans and the Missionary Movement in Africa*, edited by Sylvia M. Jacobs; and *Black Americans and the Evangelization of Africa 1877-1900*, Walter L. Williams. I have got to plug it. It's going to be my new vocation. God bless you. Thank you.

Elward Ellis, after seven and a half years with InterVarsity Christian Fellowship, has accepted the presidency of the Destiny Movement, Incorporated, which is a new mission organization committed to increasing African American involvement in the world mission of the church at home and abroad.

Ray Bakke, professor of ministry at Northern Baptist Theological Seminary, is senior and associate international coordinator for the Lausanne Committee for World Evangelization. He is also the author of The Urban Christian *(IVP).*

Floyd McClung, Jr., is executive director of international operations and director of urban missions with Youth With A Mission, a worldwide ministry training young adults in missions.

Harvie M. Conn, former missionary in Korea, is professor of missions and director of the urban missions program at Westminster Theological Seminary.

IV
The
Missionary's
Call

10
Are You a Follower of Jesus Christ?

Billy Graham

THE SIXTH CHAPTER OF THE BOOK OF ISAIAH TELLS ABOUT A DRAMATIC EVENT which not only profoundly affected the life of Isaiah, but through him eventually influenced the life of the entire nation.

In the year that King Uzziah died, I saw the Lord seated on a throne, high and exalted, and the train of his robe filled the temple. Above him were seraphs, each with six wings: With two wings they covered their faces, with two they covered their feet, and with two they were flying. And they were calling to one another:

"Holy, holy, holy is the LORD Almighty; the whole earth is full of his glory."

At the sound of their voices the doorposts and thresholds shook and the temple was filled with smoke.

"Woe to me!" I cried. "I am ruined! For I am a man of unclean lips, and I live among a people of unclean lips, and my eyes have seen the King, the LORD Almighty."

Then one of the seraphs flew to me with a live coal in his hand, which he had taken with tongs from the altar. With it he touched my mouth and said, "See, this has touched your lips; your guilt is taken away and your sin atoned for."

Then I heard the voice of the Lord saying, "Whom shall I send? And who will go for us?"

And I said, "Here am I. Send me!"

He said, "Go and tell this people." (Is 6:1-9)

A Crisis Situation

"Go and tell this people." As I think of all of you, I cannot help thinking of those 17,000 hidden people groups throughout the world. But the message I want to bring you tonight is personal. Many of you are faced with personal crises. For some of you it may be in your family; for some of you it may be the divorce of your parents or the lingering illness of someone you love. Others of you may be facing a crisis in your own personal life. It could be that a very important relationship is being broken, or perhaps a door has been closed on an opportunity that seemed to be a fulfillment of your dreams. Now you're not sure what lies ahead.

For some of you the crisis tonight is spiritual. You're struggling with a decision that will determine the direction of your life. And like Jacob, you're wrestling with God. The outcome is still in doubt. You're hoping to find the answer at Urbana this week.

Some of you are searching for that certain something that will make your life complete. You have never really committed your life totally and completely to Christ. You don't have the assurance that if you died tonight you would go to heaven. You aren't sure that your sins are forgiven. You aren't certain that you have a relationship with Christ.

Whatever your problem, I want to encourage you by saying that it can become a doorway to a new and deeper relationship with God. And it's often in a crisis of life that disappointment and pain cause us to turn our eyes toward God. In times of difficulty the scales are stripped from our eyes, and we are motivated to focus our attention on him.

Isaiah went to the temple because there was a crisis in Israel. King Uzziah had just died. For fifty-two years he had been the ruler of Judah, longer than any other king up to that time. His reign had been marked by peace and unparalleled prosperity, the greatest prosperity in Judah's history.

But now the nation was facing a series of crises. There was a political crisis. From the east there were rumors of a hostile and aggressive new king on the throne of Judah's archenemy, Assyria. There was an economic crisis. Would the material prosperity continue under Uzziah's inexperienced son? There was social crisis. Material prosperity had brought about not only great wealth, but great poverty and social injustice. And there was a spiritual crisis. In his early years Uzziah had been a godly king, but as the years went by and he became more and more successful, he became less and less interested in God's will. The Bible says, "But after Uzziah became powerful, his pride led to his downfall. He was unfaithful to the LORD his God" (2 Chron 26:16).

You and I live in a world of great uncertainty and upheaval. No matter where we look, we see signs of turmoil—political, social, economic and spiritual. Right now many of our major magazines and newspapers are running articles that look forward to the coming year. What will 1988 bring? Without exception, the ones I have read so far have been pessimistic about the new year.

Tonight there are people all over our country that are fearful of what the future might hold. We have just signed the INF treaty, but that is only one foot of progress in the hundred-yard distance between us and disarmament. As the Secretary of State said, "We still have enough bombs to blow up this planet in thirty minutes." And many nations besides the United States and the Soviet Union have nuclear weapons. Does the human race have the moral and spiritual fortitude to stop this mad race toward destruction?

Isaiah was a young man living in the midst of turmoil and uncertainty. He lived in the great city of Jerusalem, and ancient Jewish tradition says that he was related to the royal family. Maybe he had been dazzled by success and riches. Maybe he was the first Yuppie. But suddenly Isaiah realized the world would never be the same. It was going to change. A recent article in the Chicago Tribune carried this headline, "Yuppies Abandoning the Finer Things in Life for a Finer Life." The article went on to say that Yuppies are dissatisfied and disillusioned. They have quality kitchens, quality cars, quality video systems, but they have not wound up with quality lives. A great disillusionment has set in among the Yuppies.

Wherever I travel around the world I find people asking the same questions: What is the meaning and purpose of life? Where did we come from? Why are we here? Where are we going? Why is it all happening the way it is? The world's best minds have offered a bewildering array of answers. Freud says that in order for you to change, you must resolve your unconscious conflicts. Karl Marx says in order for you to change, you must help establish a classless society. Carl Jung says that in order for you to change, you must undergo the mystery of the transformation process. Carl Rogers says that in order for you to change, you must be free to be self-actualized. B. F. Skinner says that in order for you to change, you must alter your stimulus-response mechanisms.

Isaiah discovered that the most transforming thing in life is knowing God personally and doing his will. Isaiah gives us a personal and intimate account of his experience with God—an experience that in many ways can be your experience as you meet Christ and respond to his call. Let me summarize this experience in six words.

Comprehension
First there was *comprehension.* Isaiah comprehended who God is. We don't know how deep Isaiah's belief and commitment to God was before this, but now he comes to comprehend God in a new way. He comes to realize who God really is and what he is like. He has a vision of the Lord, high and lifted up, emphasizing his majesty and glory. Then he sees the seraphs who were angelic beings: "And they were calling to one another: 'Holy, holy, holy is the LORD Almighty; the whole earth is full of his glory' " (v. 3). Their threefold praise underlines the holiness and the righteousness of God, emphasizing how important it is for us to understand that God is absolutely holy, pure and righteous. The prophet Habakkuk said of God, "Your eyes are too pure to look on evil; you cannot tolerate wrong" (Hab 1:13). The Scripture tells us that unless we have that same righteousness and that same holiness we will never get to heaven.

We have lost sight of the holiness of God today. Some of you have become involved in habits or relationships that are wrong, and you have excused them and justified them because you have lost sight of the holiness of God. But the Bible warns, "Do not be deceived: God cannot be mocked. A man reaps what he sows. The one who sows to please his sinful nature, from that nature will reap destruction; the one who sows to please the Spirit, from the Spirit will reap eternal life" (Gal 6:7-8).

Christ died on the cross to provide for you the righteousness and holiness that you cannot have apart from him. When you trust in Christ for salvation, you are clothed in the righteousness of God. When God sees you, he sees the righteousness of Christ and he doesn't condemn you. What a wonderful thing!

Have you comprehended who God really is and what he is like? We can see glimpses of him in creation and in our own conscience and sometimes in the things that other people do. But we do not really see God as he is until we see him in his Word, the Bible. We know God through the Scriptures. That's the reason it's important to study the Scriptures, to meditate on them night and day. But we spend too much time watching TV or reading magazines, entertaining ourselves when we ought to be in the Scriptures. There we comprehend God in all of his holiness and righteousness.

Conviction

The second word that I want to mention is *conviction*. As soon as Isaiah saw who God really is, his immediate response was a deep conviction of his own sinfulness. " 'Woe to me!' I cried. 'I am ruined! For I am a man of unclean lips, and I live among a people of unclean lips' " (v. 5). Society around me is sick. I'm sick. Oh, God, help me!

Everyone who's ever seen a true reflection of God is deeply convicted of his own sin. When Peter saw the Lord, he said, "Depart from me, for I am a sinful man, O Lord!" (Lk 5:8 KJV). When Job saw the glory and holiness of God, he said, "I abhor myself" (Job 42:6 KJV). The closer you get to Christ, the more sinful you're going to feel. The closer you get to Christ, the more unworthy you're going to be. The fact that you're aware of your sin and feel guilty about it is a sign of spiritual light. The most dangerous condition is one in which you can no longer sense that you have drifted away from God.

A lot of what goes on today in Christian circles indicates that we've not really comprehended and experienced God as Isaiah did. We've got to the point where we have become flippant about God. We tell jokes about him. God's name is used so often in profanity in the entertainment world today, it's almost embarrassing to turn on the television set. We do not realize how this offends a holy and righteous God. We act as if it doesn't really matter how we live or what we think or say because we think God will forgive us anyway. We forget that we are on holy ground. The Bible says we all need God's forgiveness, because "all have sinned, and fall short of the glory of God" (Rom 3:23 KJV).

I came to my first Urbana in 1948—the first one they had here—they had one in Toronto before—one of the other speakers was Donald Grey Barnhouse. He was a giant of a preacher from Philadelphia, and he preached one message on hell and another on separation from the world. I'll never forget his messages on separation from the world. We have gotten away from that. We have moved in with the world and allowed the world to penetrate the way we live. So the things we used to call sin are no longer sin. Things that we would have abhorred a few years ago, we accept as a matter of fact today, not realizing that they offend a holy God.

I try to go walking or swimming every day, and as I'm walking or swimming, I find myself praying. I don't have to pray too long before I am confessing things that the Holy Spirit points out in my life that I didn't realize were there. Did you ever have that experience? Do you realize you need God's forgiveness, and you need to be reconciled to him?

Confession

Isaiah's comprehension of God and his conviction of his own sin leads to the third word that I would like to mention, and that is *confession*. In verse 5 he says, "I am a man of unclean lips, and I live among a people of unclean lips, and my eyes have seen the King, the LORD Almighty."

He was not only convicted of his sin, but he confessed it openly. Sometimes we can feel guilty, very guilty, and yet we never do anything about it because we are afraid to face it and repent of it. But God cannot use us in the way he wants to use us if we refuse to confess our sin and seek his cleansing. The Psalmist declared, "If I had cherished sin in my heart, the Lord would not have listened" (Ps 66:18).

There have been times in my life when I have been overwhelmed with conviction of my own failure and sin and have gone out alone, confessing every sin I could think of, asking God to forgive me and cleanse me so he could use me. The Bible says, "But just as he who called you is holy, so be holy in all you do; for it is written: 'Be holy, because I am holy' " (1 Pet 1:15-16). Tonight I am going to ask you to turn from whatever it is that is keeping you from Christ and to give your life without reserve to him.

Cleansing

After comprehension, conviction and confession, there was cleansing. Verse 6 says, "Then one of the seraphs flew to me with a live coal in his hand, which he had taken with tongs from the altar. With it he touched my mouth and said, 'See, this has touched your lips; your guilt is taken away and your sin atoned for.' " Notice that God provided the answer for Isaiah's sins, for a coal is taken from off the altar. All his goodness, all his heritage, all his intentions and resolutions about the future could not bring cleansing. Only God can forgive us and cleanse us, and he has provided the way. The angel took the live coal from the altar to cleanse him from sin.

When we turn to the New Testament, we understand more fully what God has done and what was foreshadowed here. The Bible says you cannot save yourself and that you and I deserve only the judgment of a holy God. But the Bible also tells us something else about God. The Bible tells us that God loves us, and the ultimate proof of his love is that he sent his only Son, Jesus Christ, into the world to die as a perfect and final sacrifice for sin.

I don't understand how God could allow his Son, his only begotten Son, to be nailed to a Roman cross. I don't understand how God in that mysterious moment took your sins and my sins and laid them on his Son. Jesus Christ had never committed immorality. He had never told a lie. He had never stolen anything. He had never had evil thoughts. All of a sudden he was guilty of it all.

"God made him who had no sin to be sin for us, so that in him we might become the righteousness of God" (2 Cor 5:21). Just think of Christ becoming sin, your sin, the things you've done, the things you've thought about, the things that are on record. Wouldn't it be wonderful to go to bed tonight and know that every sin you have ever committed has been taken care of and that you are right with the Lord?

In a great audience like this there are some of you who have never committed your lives to Jesus Christ. You cannot honestly say that you are a follower of him. Maybe you have assumed that you were, but down inside tonight you are uncertain about your relationship with God, and you know you need to make your commitment firm. Or maybe you came here for some other reason—just because someone talked you into coming, or to be with your girlfriend or boyfriend. Or perhaps you came because deep down inside of you there is an emptiness and a loneliness, and you are on a spiritual search for God. Whatever your reason, tonight Christ wants to come into your life. He wants to forgive you and cleanse you, and he wants to make you his child forever. He wants you to become his disciple, and he wants to give you a new meaning and purpose in life.

Challenge

After Isaiah's cleansing came the *challenge*. Verse eight reads, "Then I heard the voice of the Lord saying, 'Whom shall I send? And who will go for us?' "

Why did God ask that question? There are two reasons. The first reason God asked that question is because he wants men and women to come to know him, but they will never come to know him if they do not hear the gospel. God looks out on this world that is in rebellion against him, and it breaks his heart. He is not content to stand back and allow the world to continue on its way to a Christless eternity. God has done everything possible to bring a lost humanity back to himself, and he yearns to have men and women from every race and nation on earth to turn to him and come to know him. He is already speaking to people in China. He is already speaking to people in the Soviet Union. He is already speaking to people in the Middle East in ways that would amaze us if we knew about them.

About three weeks ago we received a letter from a woman who is teaching school in China. She wrote us this little story. "The other day I went out with two Japanese teachers. They asked me to join them on a trip to a mountain, a two-day journey away. On the way we passed by an old beggar sitting by the road. Something about him touched my heart and it seemed that God whispered to me, 'Go speak to him.' But I didn't do it. I decided to wait until I came back. And sure enough, on our return he was still there. I went over and I spoke to him and told him about Jesus Christ and tears came to his eyes. He said, 'You know, I've been talking to him all my life, but I didn't know his name.' "

You see, the Lord is revealing himself to people in ways you may never have dreamed of. I meet people in many parts of the world where the gospel cannot be proclaimed outside of a church, or in some cases only under severe restrictions. They tell me they listen to Transworld Radio or Far East Broadcasting. Or they have read a tract. I know a man who is the surgeon general of his country. He was walking down a street, and a piece of paper stuck to his shoe and when he got home he pulled it off in disgust. But it was about the gospel. He read it and became a Christian and has become a great Bible teacher in his country. Somebody had left a tract.

It is estimated that in China today there are between thirty and fifty million Christians. When the missionaries left in the late forties, there were estimated to be 700,000 Chinese Christians. Where did they come from? What happened in China? This massive growth of the church that has taken place in the past few decades with no public preaching, no literature, no radio, no television, no nothing. The Holy Spirit began to work. People would live the Christian life before their fellow workers and people would come and ask them, "What is the difference in your life? Little house groups began to meet. Small groups sprang up here and there. When the cultural revolution came, they went to prison and suffered for their faith. They stood for God. And now today we see evidence of the power of the gospel.

I don't believe we should all get on the plane and rush over to China as missionaries. They have already proved that by God's power they can evangelize China. Oh, we can help. We can go out as teachers and engineers. We can be supportive of the church in China either by our presence or by our prayers. But for now, let's let the Chinese build their own church. Maybe the day will come when they can send some missionaries to us, and we can send some to China. But for the present, let's not even use the word *missionary* when we're talking about China.

The second reason God asked the question "Who will go?" is that God's message demands messengers. The Bible says, "How, then, can they call on the one they have not believed in? And how can they believe in the one of whom they have not heard? And how can they hear without someone preaching to them? And how can they preach unless they are sent?" God looks upon our world today, in all of its spiritual lostness and need, and says, "Who will go for us?" Who will go to the teeming urban centers of our world? Who will go to the small villages, to the hidden peoples, to the universities, to the difficult places, to our own country? Who will declare—by word and deed—the love of Christ to those who do not know him? The challenge is to you and to me, as God would lead us and call us. You cannot remain the same once you have seen the world as God sees it, and once you have seen your life as God sees it.

Isaiah responded, "Here am I. Send me!" God had not promised Isaiah that it would be easy or glamorous or romantic or that people would praise him. I know it's great to think that we might get on a boat, or a plane, and arrive in some distant place where God will somehow fill us with his Spirit, and we will be totally different. But if you are not winning people to Christ here, if you're not serving Christ here, he can't use you there. You must witness for him here first—on your campus, in your place of work.

God is calling us to do something unique in our generation. Marcel Marceau said this, "If you want to make an impact on America, you have to do something unique." He was referring to the entertainment world. But God is calling us to do something unique, to deny ourselves, take up the cross and follow him—out among the masses that need

Christ. He is calling us to consider his call before our careers, to wrestle in prayer over the mission he has for us in life. God is calling us to look at the world and see it as he sees it and answer the question, "Who will go for us?"

Just before World War 1 a young man arrived in Cairo, Egypt. He was 25 years old, a graduate of Yale University and Princeton Seminary. He was tall, handsome, athletic, intelligent, single and very rich. His name was William Borden, and he was the heir to one of America's great fortunes. But he had turned his back on all the privilege and all the luxury and all the money that could have been his and was on his way to China as a missionary.

But shortly after arriving in Cairo he became critically ill with cerebral meningitis, and in a matter of days he was dead. Many students back in America asked, "Was it worth it?" Later his biographer wrote that Borden had said, "No reserve, no retreat, no regrets." There was no hesitation in his dedication to the Lord. What about you? *No reserve* —no holding anything back. *No regrets*—never turning back from the path God has set before you. *No regrets*—joyously knowing that God's way is always best.

There are a thousand things you can do with your life; a thousand ways you can spend it. But how many of them will enable you to say at the end of your life "no reserve, no retreat, no regrets"? There is only one way you can truly say that, and that is to be a follower of the Lord Jesus Christ.

Billy Graham, author and internationally known evangelist, has preached the gospel to millions throughout the world.

11
The Lordship of Christ

George Verwer

TURN WITH ME IN YOUR BIBLES TO THE MOST IMPORTANT COMMANDMENT IN ALL of Scripture, Mark 12:30–31. "Love the Lord your God with all your heart and with all your soul and with all your mind and with all your strength." This is the first commandment. Let's remember that. With all the other emphases, all the books, all the cassette tapes, it's easy to forget the basics. "The second is this: 'Love your neighbor as yourself.' There is no commandment greater than these."

I have wrestled with this message on the lordship of Christ more than almost any other message I've ever given. But as I was wrestling with this message and praying and reading and listening to tapes, seven words came to my heart. You are hearing so many messages here, but I would like you to write down these seven words, and I pray that if you look back at my feeble message some years down the road, you will remember these seven words.

Lordship
The first word is *lordship.* We believe in lordship at Operation Mo–

bilization, as does InterVarsity Christian Fellowship and the International Fellowship of Evangelical Students. But there are some groups that hold extreme views on this subject. Some time ago I had some of them outside of a meeting I was holding on the East Coast. They were handing out literature that contained extreme statements about lordship, implying that hardly anybody is saved except them. It's amazing how Satan can take any precious doctrine and take it to an extreme. And if you begin to move for God in these days, if you made a commitment last night, if you make a commitment in these coming evenings, Satan is going to counterattack.

It's as if Satan has two basic strategies. First of all he wants to keep you from knowing the fullness of the Spirit and the fullness of commitment to Christ as lord. And when you do begin to grow in these areas, then Satan seems to change strategy, and he tries to get you into extremism. Beware of extremism and try to find the true balance we find in Scripture.

Have you heard that cliché that goes "If Jesus Christ isn't Lord of all, he's not lord at all." When I first heard that, I thought, "Boy, that's great! Sounds great! Let's thump people on the head with that one!" But then I asked, "Is it biblical?" I'm convinced that we can come to know Christ as Savior in a moment as some did last night and as I did in Madison Square Garden at 16 years of age. And I believe you can begin to know the lordship of Christ in a second.

But I believe that in order to know the lordship of Christ in all God wants it to mean in our lives takes a lifetime. It is a lifetime of constantly growing and repenting. Praise God that his Spirit doesn't reveal to us all the self-life in one glimpse. We wouldn't be able to handle the sight. But as we grow, as we get more into the Word, as we get into various training experiences, God reveals more of our self-life, and we repent and we grow.

We need a greater emphasis on spiritual growth. You may have a crisis experience in your life. You may have a crisis this week. Hallelujah, I'm not against crises. I've had dozens of them myself.

I don't know if you've read much of A. W. Tozer, but I believe he is one of the most laser-beam writers that this country ever had. Here's what he has to say about too much enthusiasm in the church. Speaking of which, I wonder if that is the big problem in your church—too much enthusiasm, people so excited about Christ that they are always running off witnessing and neglecting the church supper. Thinking that too much enthusiasm is the greatest problem in the average church, Tozer said, is like sending a squadron of policemen to the nearby cemetery to guard against demonstrations by the residents.

I find very few people today who are memorizing the Scriptures. I find many people acknowledging they have lazy minds.

When I spoke here twenty years ago I gave an invitation for people to repent, for people to enter into a radical life-changing walk with God. Four thousand people stood up at that invitation. I've had letters from many of those people, and out of that Urbana convention came my book called *Hunger for Reality*. Over the past twenty years I have received about 15,000 letters. I have read all of them, and they have helped prepare me to speak to you tonight.

Four Areas of Lordship

First of all, I want you to examine how you use your time. Is Christ Lord of your time? How much time do you waste? I have been praying for a long time that I might do better at redeeming the time. I hate to sit in the back of a car and not do something, whether that means witnessing to someone or reading. For a Christmas gift someone gave me a flashlight device for reading in the dark. Now I can read the Word of God in the dark or wherever I go.

Second, is Christ lord over your tongue? This has been my problem. My mother wasn't a prophet, but she said when I was small, "Son, you've got a big mouth." I've hardly ever had anyone compliment me on my mouth, except once a dentist working on a back tooth said, "There's plenty of space in here."

If you, brothers and sisters, are thinking about being a crosscultural communicator, then you must deal with the sins of the tongue. As a young baby Christian I read Billy Graham's sermon on the sins of the tongue, and I repented and I cried to God and I said, "Lord if you don't change my vocabulary, if you don't do something about my impatience and my irritability, I cannot serve you." It was not until I got desperate in Mexico City, after offending my young Mexican workers, and really repented and got into God's Word that I started to get more mouth control. Don't give up. If God can give victory and change a character like me, I can tell you there is hope for everyone else.

Third, can you say that Christ is lord over your sexuality? This perhaps is the biggest battle of all. In fact, Billy Graham in 1957 said that if you don't win the battle against impurity, you lose the battle of the Christian life. I have been saying the same thing now for twenty years, especially in this country. Sexual impurity is an epidemic in the church of Jesus Christ today, and I tell you it scares me far more than AIDS.

I thank God for John White's book *Eros Defiled.* I thank God for Erwin Lutzer's book *Living with Your Passions.* And I believe that even if you have a slight struggle and problem in this area, you ought to get those books, you ought to memorize those chapters in Proverbs, and you ought to look at the many other verses in the Bible on the subject of sex. In fact, there are over 500 Scriptures about sex—even in the King James Version.

I'm going to share something with you because I think it's a grave mistake if you think that this battle is going to immediately disappear if you pray a nice prayer. In my own life I have battled my strong sexual drive all of my life. I knew as a teenager that it would either make me or break me. I knew that there was no middle ground for me. I had to be filled with the Spirit every day. I had to be crucified every day or I'd get in trouble. I would go for sin like a grasshopper for wheat, if it wasn't for the power of Jesus Christ. I want you to know that we as Christian leaders are vulnerable, we are weak, we are strugglers.

I live in London, England. I love to go in the woods and worship God. I often go for days of prayer. Several years ago I was out in the woods praising and worshiping God, and I happened to spot a ten-dollar pornographic magazine hanging in a tree. Someone had been using it for target practice. Now I'm a pornoholic, just like an alcoholic. If I stay completely away, I don't have a problem. But there I was walking in the woods, and there was this magazine in the tree.

Now, what a wonderful testimony it would be if I could stand in front of 18,000 people and tell you how George Verwer, the founder and leader of Operation Mobilization, with one laser beam of Holy-Ghost power zapped that magazine. But the truth is that magazine made a complete fool out of me. And I stand here not as the model disciple, I stand here not as a Christian leader or as a public speaker or a spiritual revolutionary, I stand here as a product of the grace of God. God uses ordinary people. You may feel that you're a failure, but that failure can be the back door to success.

Year ago I had this great vision for the Soviet Union. I had no interest in western Europe. I was concerned for the Muslim world, for Spain because it was under Franco, and for the Soviet Union. I was learning Russian. I went into the Soviet Union. I got across the border with my printing press and with my Gospels in corn-flakes boxes. Some of you know my good friend Brother Andrew, God's Smuggler. Tonight you have Brother George, God's Bungler.

The second day in the Soviet Union I was arrested by the secret police and accused of being a spy, a first-class fiasco. But I went back and spent the day in prayer in the mountains near Vienna, and there the Lord first gave me those two words, "Operation Mobilization" and the vision of European young people being renewed and mobilized to evangelize the millions across the world, reaching them with the gospel of Christ. And to some degree that has happened. See how God can use failure to open the door to success.

Fourth, can you say that the Lord Jesus Christ is Lord over your resources? Materialism doesn't leave us easily. We seem to have trouble even acknowledging it as a problem. It's always the other guy that's more materialistic than us. A. W. Tozer said materialism will not be overcome by raising your hand. It will depart from you like a tooth being extracted from your jaw. My dear brothers and sisters, if we don't deal with materialism in the church, if we don't deal with it in our own lives and put our resources and our money on the altar, and use them as God would have us use them, then I don't believe we will reach those unreached people.

Six More Words to Live By
You may ask what some of those other words are that burn upon my heart. The second one is simply *honesty.* I give a plea for honesty and integrity. In our publicity, in our conversation with one another, let's not pretend to be spiritual if we know we are not. Let's be in honest fellowship with one another and share and confess our sins.

The third word is *reality*—reality with God. Knowing God must be our first priority, even more important than world missions. Read some of those great books by men like A. W. Tozer, Andrew Murray and J. I. Packer.

The fourth word is *purity*—a subject that we already touched on. We talked about Christ being Lord over our sexual life. Often when we talk about purity we are reminded of David. Praise God for the forgiveness we see in David. It needs to be emphasized. But for young people I've got someone more exciting than David.

Those of you who are just beginning your life, consider Joseph. Joseph—that's the guy that challenges me. He challenges me to stick as closely as I can to Plan A. Plan A means that you live a life of purity before God and man from the moment of your conversion. Joseph was tempted by this voluptuous beauty—I don't even like to imagine it. Joseph was lonely, he was a man, but he said, "I will not do this wicked thing." And he wins the victory. Now we always think, Well, when you win a victory like that, you get a reward, right? You get a lovely Christian girlfriend the next day. No, no, he got prison. And that was before co-education.

The fifth word I leave with you is *discipline.* In 1 Corinthians 9 Paul says, "I buffet my body and bring it into subjection." Without discipline we aren't going to go very far because the way ahead is going to be rough, and it is going to be tough.

The sixth word is *vision.* Let's pray now that God will increase our vision for the whole world, for the fields that are ripe unto harvest.

And finally, the seventh word, my favorite word, *action.* If you believed this roof were going to fall in, what would you do? Write a little chorus about falling roofs? Have a theological discussion about falling roofs? No. If you believed that this roof were going to fall in, you would move, you would mobilize. If we believed right now that a fire was starting right underneath this building as we had underneath the escalator system in the London subway recently, what would we do? We would move. Brothers and sisters, the world is on fire. The harvest is plenteous; the laborers are few. Satan is trying to hinder us on every side. Let us rise up. Let us mobilize and let us go forth making Jesus Christ absolute Lord every day of our life.

George Verwer is founder and director of Operation Mobilization, a missionary training ministry active on every continent.

12
Knowing the Will of God

Roberta Hestenes

MY FIRST MISSIONARY CONFERENCE CAME ABOUT THREE MONTHS AFTER MY conversion. I went off into the mountains of Southern California to learn about knowing the will of God. When I came home from that conference, my friends dropped me off at the door of my home and I walked into that house of unbelieving parents and an alcoholic father. My father said to me that night in bitterness and anger and rage, "If you're going to hang out with those kind of people, if that's the kind of thing you want to do with your life, I don't want you here anymore— get out." And I did. And I wept. And I thought about the choices. And I went to my InterVarsity group, and they loved me and took me in. They cared for me and shared with me that to do the will of God is joy. And it is.

The Joy and Toughness of Knowing God's Will
I have now walked with Jesus for twenty-nine years, and I've got something to tell you. Knowing the will of God is tough. But it is a joy. It's an adventure. I have found myself in the strangest places asking myself, "How in the world did I get here and what am I doing?"

I was in the Philippines, riding in a jeep with three sisters. We were driving round and round the central square of the city. There were some soldiers sitting on a bench, guns near at hand. And the wind was blowing the sisters' habits. We went around once, we went around twice, and then we went around three times.

I finally asked, "Why are we driving in circles around the city's center?" The sister who was driving said to me cheerfully, "Oh, that's so they won't shoot us as if we have just come down from the mountain. They shot two people last week." And I was sitting there thinking, "What am I doing here?" I was there to see the work that God was doing—a work with the poor, the marginalized, the dispossessed—people that nobody cares about, and yet God cares about. And so there I was.

Shortly after that I found myself in Ethiopia, at the height of the famine. I had been there before, so I steeled myself for what I would see there. The camp we visited had about 75,000 people who had streamed out of the mountains. Their cattle had died. The seed corn had been eaten. Drought had stripped the land bare, and they had nothing. The old and the feeble had died on the way to the camp. So I steeled myself. But they handed me a child—a baby it seemed to me—he seemed no more that eighteen months old. When I took him in my arms, I asked the mother, through the translator, "How old is your baby?" The mother, her beautiful face thin and emaciated, breasts barren and clothes torn, answered, "He is six."

Six years old—yet so malnourished, so vulnerable to the diseases that we in America inoculate our children against without even thinking twice. But in the Two-thirds World, children die today of measles, of chicken pox, of dysentery and of diarrhea. As I held that baby who wasn't a baby, I wept. I had said to myself, "I will not cry. You're not supposed to cry. You're a woman, and it's particularly important that you don't cry." And I tried to hide the tears because I was embarrassed. But the next day, as I was being introduced to a group of African relief workers, to my astonishment I heard the brother say to the group, "Friends, our sister has wept. Receive her." And they opened their hearts to me.

Many years ago there was a blind beggar who sat by the side of the road, and as the traffic went by no one paid much attention to him. But one day he heard the noise of a crowd, and he knew that something was happening. Someone important was passing by. He asked, "What's happening? What's going on?" The bystanders replied,

"It's Jesus of Nazareth. He's coming. He's on his way with his disciples to Jerusalem." Then the beggar cried out, "Jesus, son of David, have mercy on me." Luke tells us that the leaders, the ones who preceded Jesus, probably meaning the disciples, said to this beggar, "Shut up. Be quiet. Don't disturb the status quo."

All too often I sense that we are afraid to feel the hurt, the pain and the suffering of this world. We anesthetize ourselves. We keep ourselves inundated with sensations and with noise and with activities so we won't see the pain of this world. Jesus' disciples were walking down the road, and Jesus had important things to do. They were important people because they were with Jesus, and who's got time for blind beggars? But the blind man would not shut up. He cried out even louder, "Jesus, son of David, have mercy on me." And Jesus did something astonishing. He stopped, and everyone with him had to stop—why go if Jesus isn't going with you? Then Jesus called to the man. In the midst of the press of the multitude and the dust and the noise of the crowd, Jesus had time for one person's hurt.

We have a motto at World Vision. "How do you feed a hungry world? One person at a time." One by one by one. One meal given up. One contribution made. One life committed. And the world changes. Jesus healed the blind man, and the world learned to care for blind beggars.

It has been said that God loves you and has a wonderful plan for your life, and that is true. But it is even more crucial that you understand a more foundational truth, that God loves the world and has a wonderful plan for its future. The challenge before us, as we seek to know the will of God, is to understand how you and I fit into what God wants to accomplish in this world. He wants the world to know his love and righteousness. The most important thing in our lives is not to find the best job at the best salary with the most prestige and the most perks. The most important thing in our lives is to find our place in God's plan for a needy world.

We echo God's purpose every time we pray "Thy kingdom come, thy will be done on earth as it is in heaven." Do you realize how radical that prayer is? Do you realize how revolutionary you are when you pray that prayer? That prayer expresses your discontent with the status quo. When you look at the world, you don't like it and God doesn't like it. God wants to do something to change it, and he wants to do it through you and me.

How do you know the will of God? First by entering into the heart of God. Bob Pierce, as an evangelist in Korea, said when a child was thrust into his arms, "Let my heart break with the things that break the heart of God"—the blind beggars, the unwanted children, the invisible women. Jesus' disciples were astonished that he took time for a woman and taught her. But she became the first evangelist to share the good news of the Messiah with her people.

We learn the will of God by looking deeply and intensely and repeatedly at Jesus. We learn it by praying as Jesus taught us to pray. We learn it by living as Jesus showed us to live. We learn it by caring as Jesus gives us eyes to see, eyes to see people not as competitors, not as rivals, not as nuisances, not as problems, but as people that God loves. We know the will of God when we go as Jesus sent us to go when he said, "As the Father sent me, so I send you."

Some First Principles

Well and good, you say. That's good for everybody, but what about me? How do I know the will of God with my genes and chromosomes, with my history and family, my likes and dislikes, my anxieties and my joys. Me. How do I know what it is that God wants me to do. What major? What career? What organization? What spouse? What task? I taught a class at Fuller Seminary for a number of years on foundations of the spiritual life. I always asked the students if they would write something about themselves and then at the end give me prayer requests. It's interesting that over thirteen years the most common prayer request among students was to know the will of God for their future. The second most common request was that God might please send a spouse! I liked the honesty and the straightforwardness of that.

Let me first clear away some underbrush. First of all, I think God has a sense of humor. I was asked if I would talk about knowing the will of God a year and a half to two years ago. At the time I thought, "Oh, I understand that. I remember all the sermons I've ever heard on knowing the will of God." You know, you get the three harbor lights lined up— prayer, circumstances and people—and you just sail right in.

Then God did the funniest thing. I got an invitation to leave my job at Fuller and go and be the president at Eastern College. It just blew me away. I thought to myself, "What? Who, me? Are you sure?" And I went into an agony of decision making that lasted for over nine months. And here I thought I could tell you that if you follow some

handy-dandy formula with three nice steps, you could get this thing
worked out just like that. But that has not been my experience. Sometimes things click, and it's easy and clear. Other times you struggle
and you wrestle and you sweat and you pray and you ask and you
wait, and it still doesn't come. And so you do it all over again, until
it does become clear.

For some of us, our quest to know the will of God can be a search
for a blueprint, a guarantee that will give us security. But God almost
never gives us that. Our security is not in a plan. There is no computer
printout that's going to tell you what God wants to do with the rest
of your life. Our security and confidence is in a person and a relationship. The person is Jesus Christ. Our confidence comes in being followers of the way and joining in the adventure. The journey of following God is a genuine adventure, not a Disneyland ticket. We don't
know precisely how it's going to turn out. While we know that our
ultimate future with God is secure, the twists and turns along the way
hold genuine surprises for us. We will not see the whole path all at
once, but the one or two steps that we do see are enough for us to
move in the direction God wants us to go.

A second assumption that I make is that many times my need is
not to know a new truth from God, but to practice the truth that I
already know. That is hard. You don't have to ask God if he wants
you to be holy. He does. Whatever the future is, you know that God
is calling you to holiness. You don't have to ask God if he wants you
to be a witness. He does. You don't have to ask God if you should
give of your resources to further his around the world. He does. To
practice the truth that we know is the challenge that many of us have
yet to tackle sufficiently. We want more truth. But we need power,
we need courage, we need the indwelling fullness of the Holy Spirit
to live out what we know already. That will prepare us for the next
chapter of life.

Another foundational truth is that there are times in our lives when
we do not know the next step. I have discovered the hard way that
it is O.K. not to know, that we can live in the unknowing. We don't
have to have all the answers at any given moment in order to be able
to trust in God's presence and provision as we move out into the
future. Now that's scary. I would rather have it all neatly spelled out
than to face the uncertainty of waiting.

John and I were headed off to graduate school. We had three babies, and I was anxious about the move. We had been told that John

had the promise of a job in Seattle. When security clearance came through on the job, the company would move us. We just had a few things. John had had his first paying job, but it had only lasted a year before he decided to go back to graduate school. So we waited to hear from the company. I set a date in my head—it was a Friday. We would have to have God's answer by then or else . . . Now I never figured out what the other part was, but I think it was, "or else we'll have to take care of it ourselves."

So the days went by. The security clearance did not come through, and I was getting more and more anxious. I finally decided on Wednesday that God wasn't coming through, and I would have to take care of this thing myself. So I put an ad in the local paper for everything we owned. On Friday the vultures came and cleaned us out—the refrigerator, the washer, the dryer, the secondhand couch, the used cabinets. There wasn't very much there, but it was everything we owned. And at the end of the day, about five o'clock, I was sitting on the floor of our empty house when the phone rang. Now we had realized on this sale about one dollar on a hundred in terms of replacement value when we got to Seattle. But can you trust God? He hadn't come through. At 5:01 the phone rang. It was the company in Seattle. "Your security clearance is here. We are ready to send the moving truck on Monday." But I couldn't wait. Don't set dates for God! He has his own timetable, and it's a good one. You can trust him, and you don't have to have your own plan. You can go with God.

Sometimes preparation and waiting are the hardest times. I have a little poem that I put under the glass of my desk when I was in college. It reads like this,

Yet in meek duty to abide
for many a year at Mary's side,
nor heed the restless spirits ask,
"What, has the Christ forgot his task?"

Sometimes we have to wait.

The lessons of pride and humility are learned the hard way. James 4:6 tells us that "God opposes the proud but gives grace to the humble." As I have worked with hundreds of seminary students over the years, one of the things I have noticed is the dangerous tendency to set conditions on God, saying, "I will go if you provide the right spouse, the right working conditions, the right plan, the right benefits." At the age of twenty-five we have to have sixty-five figured out before we are willing to launch out. We are proud. We are dictating to God the terms on which we will enter his service. But God opposes the proud and gives grace to the humble.

The first time I went to an InterVarsity camp was at Campus by the Sea on Catalina Island. I drew my first assignment, and it was latrine duty. Now I'm a city girl, and I had grown up believing that God created the world complete with flush toilets! I struggled with that assignment. But now I reflect on the goodness of God because in cleaning those latrines I got ready for something that happened in Africa.

I was on out on the plain of the Rift Valley with the Masai people. We were having a wonderful time seeing how God is working mightily among the Masai. We heard the stories of a man who invited us into his home. His wife had given us tea—actually his three wives had given us tea—as he shared how God had come into the emptiness of his life and made him new. Turning to my husband, he said, "My house is yours, my cattle are yours, my wives are yours." And I said, "Wait a minute!"

Now this home was nothing but a dung-plastered hut with a thorn-railed cattle corral to keep the lions out. And lo, in the middle of the night, I had a need. And I got up, and I left the little hut, going out to where the lions were. There I remembered my Campus-by-the-Sea training and thought it wasn't tough enough for life out there. We must be available for whatever God wants us to do, whether it be humble or great, with a title or without, with pay or without. If God calls, it is good. And we want to do it.

Some Practical Advice

But now for some warnings centered around four words: disobedience, desires, double-mindedness and discrepancy.

Disobedience. There was a guy who once said to me, "I have never felt closer to God since I started sleeping with my girlfriend." Nonsense! He was confusing hormones with holiness. Disobedience puts a barrier between us and God, and we do not hear him as we ought.

Desires. We need to be careful not to confuse our own desires with the will of God. Because I want something desperately, because I want him or her desperately, because I want that job or that position desperately, does not make it the will of God. We live in a feel-good culture, and sometimes we are taught that knowing the will of God is getting the desires of your heart and feeling good about everything. We get the impression that when everything lines up and we are really wired, then it has got to be God's will. But consider Jesus in the garden of Gethsemane. I don't think it felt good to him, but it was the will of God.

Double-mindedness. Augustine once prayed, "Lord, make me holy, but not yet." Lord, show me your will, but not until I've had some time to bum around a while, to find myself, to do my thing, to try some things out. We won't find God's will that way. We must give ourselves to God with single-mindedness of purpose.

Discrepancy. Beware of using the wrong means to achieve the right ends. A friend said to me, "I cheated on a test, but I had to because I have to have the grades to get into medical school because God wants me to be a missionary doctor." Well, God may want him to be a missionary doctor, but he has got his means wrong. We must pursue holiness and righteousness as we move towards the end to which God has called us.

We must not exploit people in order to achieve our goals. People are to be loved, to be served, to be nourished; they are not to be climbed over. I know a man who said, "I believe God wants me to be single, but I have all these strong needs." So he got engaged to a girl, exploited her, and then left her at the end of the school year in the name of God and a high and holy purpose. But his means were not high, nor were they holy.

In a culture numbed by noise, addicted to activity and seduced by success, what do we need? We need a pattern of spiritual discipline. We need a life of prayer—not foxhole prayer—but prayer that includes listening to God as he speaks in the still small voice. We need to search the Scriptures. We need to live in a community where we are connected to brothers and sisters whose counsel we value. We need to test our spiritual gifts and abilities. We need to look at our circumstances. We need the inner witness of the Holy Spirit. And as we pray, as we study, as we live together, as we try our gifts, we begin to discover this is the way that God wants us to work.

Let me give you some questions to ask when you're seeking the will of God. They are questions I have found helpful when I am trying to determine his will.

Will it honor God?

Will it help people?

Is it worth doing?

Can it be done with integrity and holiness?

Do I have the gifts and abilities needed?

Have I listened to wise counsel?

Do I have an open door?

If we ask these questions as a yielded people, as those who pray and study and live together, we will discover that what Jesus said is true: "I have placed before you an open door that no one can shut." The will of God is a glorious thing. It's a painful thing. But it is God who is with us on the journey as we serve him. Amen.

Roberta Hestenes, former associate professor of Christian formation and discipleship at Fuller Theological Seminary, is president of Eastern College and chairperson of the board of directors of World Vision International.

13
Motivation
For World
Missions

Helen Roseveare

OUR SUBJECT FOR TONIGHT IS MOTIVATION FOR WORLD MISSION, AND I TAKE AS
my text 1 Corinthians 2:

> When I came to you, brothers, I did not come with eloquence or
> superior wisdom as I proclaimed to you the testimony about God.
> For I resolved to know nothing while I was with you except Jesus
> Christ and him crucified. I came to you in weakness and fear, and
> with much trembling. My message and my preaching were not
> with wise and persuasive words, but with a demonstration of the
> Spirit's power, so that your faith might not rest on men's wisdom,
> but on God's power.

Now to verse 9:

> As it is written:
>> "No eye has seen,
>>> no ear has heard,
>> no mind has conceived
>>> what God has prepared for those
>>> who love him." (1 Cor 2:1-5, 9)

I believe that is a wonderful summary of the book of Jonah, where God prepared the storm, prepared the great fish, prepared the great city, and prepared a common weed, a tiny worm and a severe wind in order to make Jonah the messenger he wanted him to be.

Paul continues:

But God has revealed it to us by his Spirit.

The Spirit searches all things, even the deep things of God. For who among men knows the thoughts of a man except the man's spirit within him? In the same way no one knows the thoughts of God except the Spirit of God. We have not received the spirit of the world but the Spirit who is from God, that we may understand what God has freely given us. This is what we speak, not in words taught us by human wisdom but in words taught by the Spirit, expressing spiritual truths in spiritual words. The man without the Spirit does not accept the things that come from the Spirit of God, for they are foolishness to him, and he cannot understand them, because they are spiritually discerned. The spiritual man makes judgments about all things, but he himself is not subject to any man's judgment:

"For who has known the mind of the Lord
    that he may instruct him?"

But we have the mind of Christ. (1 Cor 2:10-16)

I believe that this is the answer to our question "What will motivate us to world mission?" I believe the answer is having the mind of Christ.

Now let me ask you, How much does the world around you really matter to you? I mean the student next to you, in class or in the dormitory, the person you pass in the corridor, the one who sits next to you on public transportation. I don't mean the ones beside you here at Urbana; they are fairly easy to get along with. They are fairly respectable, aren't they? It's the other ones. How much do they matter?

And I'm not yet thinking of the 3 billion people who have never yet heard of Jesus, though each one of them matters to God. Not only do they matter to God, they are breaking God's heart. As Billy Graham said on Sunday evening, Isaiah overheard the Trinity discussing the world's needs and saying, "Whom shall we send and who will go for us?" Maybe they, the Trinity, want to send you far away or perhaps near at hand. But one thing is certain. They want to send you to those who matter so desperately to them.

One morning in 1972, just before I left the mission field, I had the shattering privilege of meeting an African at a roadside in Uganda. After the customary greetings and courtesies, as he stood and looked at me, I asked him what he wanted. He said to me in Swahili, "Are you a sent one?"

Startled by his question, I thought quickly that this is what the word *missionary* means, and I said to him, "Yes, I am, but it depends, sent by whom for what?"

And he said to me, "Are you a sent one by a great God to tell me about something called Jesus."

I confess I gasped. "Can you read?" I asked him.

"No," he answered. He was an ordinary herdsman caring for the family's cattle. I took from the car a five-colored wordless book that we use to help those who cannot read understand the way of salvation. And in the early-morning sunshine I sat beside him and had the unique joy of leading him to the Lord Jesus Christ.

That incident had involved a 6,000-mile journey from the U.K. to Zaire, and then a further 300-mile journey to the neighboring country of Uganda. But God may want you to speak to someone almost next door to you.

A few years ago as I was returning home from the city, I bought my ticket at the railway station. I had a twenty-minute journey to make, and it was pouring rain, as it usually does in my country. As I stood on the railroad platform with my umbrella up, a woman came to join me. She did not have an umbrella, so I offered to share mine. She was a captive audience then. She wasn't going to run away; it was raining hard. I thought quickly, "How can I start a conversation with her?"

On the other side of the railway tracks was a large advertisement for cigarettes. I said to her, "That makes me angry." I tell you, she was pretty angry with me for speaking to her, since in Britain you don't speak to unknown people until you've been introduced. When she quieted down a bit, I said "Well, you see, I happen to be a doctor. That poster makes young people want to smoke. Smoking causes lung cancer. Lung cancer causes death." And right there on the railway platform she broke down and cried.

The train came in, and I asked if it was hers. I helped her in and sitting beside her, I asked if I could help. She said, "I've just come from the city hospital where I went for a medical checkup, and they told me I am dying of lung cancer because I have smoked all my life." As

I realized God's overruling of our conversation, I heard her add, "And I don't know where I'm going."

I didn't know where I was going. I took out a small pocket Bible inside of which I had a little tiny copy of that same five-colored wordless book. True, I blushed from ear to ear because the whole compartment listened in while I shared with her—a respectable, upper-class white lady in the middle of Belfast—the exact same way of salvation that I had taught an illiterate herdsman on an African roadside. There was no difference.

It doesn't matter whether I travel 6,000 miles or just twenty minutes from home. That has nothing to do with it. What matters is whether the people we meet matter to us as much as they matter to God. I have to ask myself, What will make me care? What will make them matter to me? What will motivate me to share Jesus with them?

World Conditions
As I began to look at this subject, I thought, first of all, we need to know something of the condition of the world we live in. I can tell you of the appalling condition of this hell-bound world. We can speak of mounting unemployment, hunger and poverty on an unprecedented scale. We can speak of more than 3,000 unreached people groups who have never yet heard the name of Jesus, never mind whether they have heard enough to make a decision for Christ.

May I give you a quick bird's-eye view of the world in which you and I live today? There are more than one billion teenagers in our world today who are turning to drugs, occultism and the like. There are more than 900 million atheists, not only in Russia and China, but in my own country of Britain. We are living in a post-Christian era. There are more than 800 million Muslims—militant, fanatical, hard—and desperately needy of the gospel of our Lord Jesus Christ.

There are more than 700 million Roman Catholics, so near to the truth and yet not realizing that they can know a personal savior, Jesus Christ, the one mediator between God and man. There are more than 600 million high-caste Hindus—educated, yes, but with no sense of need. There are more than 500 million Buddhists, good-living and ethical, yet essentially atheistic and maybe the hardest to reach with the gospel of Jesus. And there are more than 400 million Protestants—indifferent, weak, apathetic, selfish—maybe the biggest hindrance to the advance of the gospel today.

There are more than 300 million occultists, idol worshipers, animists and spiritists. And into this world God has chosen to place 200 million born-again Christians. But before you start rejoicing and praising the Lord for what he is doing in many parts of the world, I want you to stop a minute and think. What are we doing—all 200 million of us? If ten per cent of Christians were involved in missionary work, I tell you we wouldn't be here tonight. We'd all be in glory. The job would be finished.

Not only do we not have ten per cent, we don't have one per cent, we don't have even 0.1 per cent of born-again Christians involved in missionary outreach. We can tell you of the needs of the world, we can throw figures at you, we can let you know the desperation of the world, and it doesn't move us. People talk to me about closing doors. Closing doors? That is a lie of the devil. We have more open doors today than we have ever had. God doesn't have any problem with closing doors. His problem is open doors with no one to go through them. God's problem isn't closing doors, it's closing hearts. God wants your wills to get you moving. But it doesn't work. Statistics and world conditions are not touching us.

The Content of the Gospel

So what will move us? Maybe we will be moved if we look again at the content of the gospel. I can remind you again of John 3:16: "For God so loved the world that he gave his one and only Son, that whoever believes in him shall not perish but have eternal life." Or 2 Peter 3:9: "The Lord is . . . not wanting anyone to perish, but everyone to come to repentance." You know the content of the gospel. That Christ died for your sins and mine. You know he is the only perfect and satisfactory substitute, the Lamb of God that takes away the sins of the world. You know God is holy, therefore he must condemn sin, and yet he loves the sinner. He planned redemption for all of us. There is no one else who could pay the price for sin. He alone could unlock the gate of heaven and let us in.

Are you equally certain that those outside of the gospel are lost and are going to a Christless eternity? If that is not true, Jesus never had to die. You cannot accept your salvation by the blood of Jesus if you don't believe that those outside are lost. What God in his grace and mercy does is God's affair, but God has given to us his Word, and we have to accept the fact that from our perspective the lost are lost until they come to know Christ. God has told us in Psalm 91 and Romans 1 that all men could come to know him, therefore they are without excuse. Yet all men have sinned and come short of the glory of God, and the wages of sin is death. Yet somehow their lostness doesn't motivate us.

Coming out of the supermarket one Wednesday, I spoke to a sad-looking woman ahead of me in the check-out line. She was obviously annoyed with me for speaking, but after she calmed down, I tried again. I spoke about the weather and that didn't please her either. Finally, in despair I touched her on the arm and said, "Dear, has anyone ever told you that Jesus loves you?"

She broke down. I helped her through the line, and we paid our bills. She waited at the door with her two children and her goods and my goods while I went out to get my car. Later, over coffee, she told me the most pathetic story I've ever sat and listened to. But it was her last comment that hurt me most. She said, "No one has ever told me that *anyone* loved me."

She could have heard eight years ago if I had spoken. She and I shop in the same supermarket every Wednesday. We line up at the same cash register every Wednesday morning. And because I hadn't the spunk to open my lips and speak to her of Jesus, she had not heard. I was afraid I'd be laughed at and snubbed. I didn't care enough, so she didn't hear. It isn't the content of the gospel that is going to move us to witness.

The Command of Christ

What will motivate you for mission? The condition of the world doesn't, the content of the gospel doesn't. Maybe the actual command of Christ will, "Go into all the world and preach the good news to all creation." This has been the purpose of God all through the Scriptures. In Genesis 12 he calls Abraham out from Ur of the Chaldees and tells him that all the families of the earth, all ethnic groups, will be blessed through him. All the way through all the Old Testament—Elijah, Elisha, Jonah—all of them proclaimed the word of the Lord to foreigners.

At the end of Matthew God's clear command is to go and make disciples of all ethnic groups. Jesus himself said in John 20:21, "As the Father has sent me, I am sending you." And he sends all of us who know and love him. Somewhere along the line we have got to respond to that command. If Jesus Christ is Lord of your life and mine, we have a imperative placed upon us. It's no optional extra. It's no matter of choice. It is an explicit command to go as the Father sent the Son.

Where did God the Father send the Son? Into our world of lost sinners. That is where he is sending us. Why did God the Father send his Son? To seek and to save the lost, not just to have fellowship and enjoyment with the saved. And God is sending us out to do the same. How did God send his son? As a slave willing to die on Calvary. That is how he wishes to send you and me out—as his slaves, willing to die to ourselves, our ambitions, our wants and our feelings. He sends us out as Jesus was sent out for us, so that others might come to the Father.

When Jesus was feeding the 5,000, the disciples came to him and said, "Send them away." He said, "No, you feed them." It doesn't say in the Greek "You feed them with something or other." It just says "You feed them." "You give yourselves to them to be fed." No matter how you read it, there is nothing given to feed them—only you. In John's Gospel he says, "I am the bread of life," and he gave his life on Calvary to feed a needy world. We are the church, we are his body, and we are the bread of life. He said, "Go out and feed them, with yourselves, with all that you are and all that you have, and all I'll give through you."

The Mind of Christ

But this command of Jesus doesn't stir us to do anything. When you are stirred emotionally, you ought to do something. But by the time you get back to the university, back into the grind of everyday studies, the Urbana atmosphere won't be with you and things will look different. It's not only that the condition of the world doesn't budge us or that the content of the gospel doesn't budge us, but even the command of Christ doesn't budge us. You say, "Oh, I know that someone is going to tell them, someone is going to feed them, but not me." And we sit at home. What will make us obey and care and go to the waiting millions?

The answer is that we must have the character of God—the mind of Christ. In despair I ask myself, and I ask you, Does Jesus Christ live in me? Does he live in you? Have I actually got the very character of God himself, this God who loves all men, the God who doesn't want any to perish? Is he so indwelling me that he is loving through me, thinking through me, acting through me? Am I motivated by the indwelling Christ? If not, are you willing to move on to what I call a

Galatians 2:20 experience?

When Paul wrote to the Galatians, they were not supermature saints. They were not people who had been on the journey for a long time and were getting up to the stage where they thought they needed a second blessing. They were babes in Christ. They had about ten days of preaching from Paul on his first missionary journey, maybe another ten on his second missionary journey, and then he wrote to them this letter. He wrote, "I have been crucified with Christ and I no longer live, but Christ lives in me" (Gal 2:20). That was to be their everyday Christian experience—not I, but Christ living in me.

I had been on the mission field four years when God began to open my eyes to the wonderful truth of Galatians 2:20. Things had gone pretty badly, and I had all of the excuses I needed. I was desperately overworked. I was the only doctor for half a million patients. There was no colleague to turn to, and all the responsibility fell on my shoulders. I had become quick-tempered and impatient with my colleagues—Africans and missionaries alike.

Fortunately for me my African pastor was watching me and saw my spiritual need. One Friday he came to my village and told me to pack my bags; I was going to spend some time in his village. I packed my rucksack, got my bicycle and cycled out behind him to his village. He had told his wife I was coming, and she had a room ready for me. Firmly, but courteously he said, "Just get yourself in there and get yourself straight with God."

Friday night, all day Saturday, Saturday night, all day Sunday, I spent before God. And I got nowhere. The heavens were like brass, the Bible was dead, I couldn't get through to him. By Sunday night I was depressed and discouraged, I had such a sense of failure—everything was so hopeless. I went to the door of the house and out in the courtyard, by the embers of the fire, sat my pastor and his wife. I went out and sat beside them. After a long, painful silence, I said, "Please, help me." Pastor leaned towards me and spoke patiently, "Helen, do you know what's wrong with you? We can see so much Helen that we cannot see Jesus."

He was silent for a while. And then, with his heel he drew a large capital *I* in the dirt. Then quietly and deliberately he said to me, "I think you know that person, don't you? *I* dominates your life. Me, my, mine, self—everything revolves around you—your program, your vision, what you want to do. Even when you hear on the news that some new law has been passed, the first thing you ask is, How will that disrupt my program? *I* is in the middle of everything."

He said some other things that were very painful for me to take. I knew they were true, but I didn't realize he did. And then he seemed to change the conversation. He said, "I notice that you drink a lot of coffee, and every time they bring you a cup of coffee you stand with it in your hand waiting for it to cool. May I suggest to you that everytime you stand waiting for your cup of coffee to cool you just pray a short prayer. And as he said the words of the prayer, he moved his foot across the dirt. "May I suggest that you pray, 'Please God, cross out the *I.* "

Simplified theology, isn't it? The crossed-out-*I*-life. I think that is what Paul meant when he said, "I have been crucified with Christ and I no longer live, but Christ lives in me" (Gal 2:20). Although my experience took place over thirty years ago, I still pray that prayer as God reminds me, "Please God, cross out the *I.* Then Jesus can take over and live in me. We are all called to be partakers of the very nature of God. We are called to have his mind, to be Christlike, to be sold out to him, transformed into his likeness, with our minds renewed by the Holy Spirit so that we think and see and care as he does. And as this happens we will inevitably be missionaries—because he is. We cannot escape it.

God yearns that all men should come to know him as savior. When you have the mind of Christ you will be caught up in the great program of God that runs from Genesis 12 where he says to Abraham, "All peoples on earth will be blessed through you," right through to Revelation 7:9 where we see people of all tongues and nations and kindred and people worshiping the lamb. The only thing that links the promise to Abraham and the fulfillment of Revelation is the command "Go and make disciples of all nations." This is Gód's consuming passion, and it will take possession of you and drive you out into the world.

That is the power of the indwelling character of almighty God. He alone can motivate us into action. When we have the mind of Christ, we will find we must obey the command of Jesus. Then the compassion of Jesus takes over, and we begin to weep for the condition of the world.

I know that I want to have the mind of Christ. When I read of the Trinity saying, "Who will go for us?" (Is 6:8), I want to say, "Lord, here am I, should you ever find it in your will and purpose, should you ever give me the privilege of going for you." What are you holding back on? What keeps you from yielding to him?

What's Your Horse?

I was speaking at a church in Melbourne, Australia, and there were a good number of students in the congregation. At the end of the meeting the pastor who knew his congregation very well, said, "As we sing the last hymn, I want to challenge you all. If you're holding back on God for something that you know you should have given to God but have not been willing to, will you come forward? I don't want you to tell me what it is, will you just tell God? Tell him, 'I take my hands off—it's yours.' " Then he mentioned several obstacles: "I'll go Lord, but I want to be married first." "I'll go Lord, but I want to get that extra degree."

During the singing of the hymn, they began coming forward—not many, but a few. In the front row there were three girls, eleven, thirteen and fifteen years of age, and I watched them. The thirteen-year-old obviously wanted to come forward, but she didn't. So at the end of the hymn I went down to speak to her, but she had shot out a side door. She didn't want to be caught by me!

So I sat down where she had been and started talking to the ladies behind me. One of these was an American and she was almost heart-broken. "Can you help me?" she asked. "What's the matter?" I asked. She said, "My husband and I came out here to Australia as missionaries to the aborigines. We were asked to do work in downtown Melbourne first, in order to get acclimatized.

"We have two daughters, one is thirteen and the other fifteen. The fifteen-year-old settled in at once without any problems. But the thirteen-year-old," she began to stammer, "is tearing us apart. She's destroying our family, and she's destroying our fellowship." Nearly in tears she asked, "Is it right for my husband and me to force our call to be missionaries on our children?"

I was praying desperately, asking God for the answer. I didn't know what to say, but at that moment she added, "At home we lived on Grandmama's farm and our thirteen-year-old had a horse."

Just at that moment two children came to the end of the pew, and I guessed that one of these was the thirteen-year-old. So I turned and said "Good evening." One of them said "Good evening" and the other said "Hi." Now I knew that one was Australian and the other American. I chatted with the Australian to set the other girl at ease and then turned to the American lass and said, "You're a stranger here, aren't you?"

"Yes," she responded.

"Not easy to live in another country?"

"No."

And we had a monosyllabic conversation. Just then the pastor called me to shake hands with people in the back. I went, but when everyone had left, I went up to the front to get my Bible. There the thirteen-year-old met me eyeball to eyeball.

"Was I too young to come forward tonight?" she asked.

"No, I thought you wanted to, didn't you?"

"Yes."

"OK, let's go now."

So we went forward together and knelt on the steps by the platform. I said, "What do you want to give to Jesus?" No answer.

"Go on, you just tell Jesus in your own words what you want to give to him." The little girl began to sob, her whole body shaking. I put my arm around her and said, "Just tell him in your own words."

After a terrible struggle she burst out, "My horse!"

I said "OK, darling, let's give the horse to Jesus."

And we prayed together, and we gave the horse to Jesus. Then she looked up at me with a gorgeous smile and tears pouring down her cheeks, "Oh," she said, "my mom and dad are going to be so pleased about this. I've made their life hell."

"OK," I said, "are you going to make their life heaven?"

"I sure am," she answered, "I want them to be the very best missionaries for Jesus."

Listen, a thirteen-year-old had caught the point. Do you have a horse? Before you go to sleep tonight will you give it to Jesus—and get moving for God?

Helen Roseveare, author of Give Me This Mountain *and* He Gave Us a Valley, *served as a medical missionary in Zaire from 1953 to 1973 with World Evangelical Crusade International.*

14
The Urgency of the Call

Tony Campolo

TWO THOUSAND YEARS AGO, THEY NAILED OUR JESUS TO THE CROSS. TWO thousand years ago, they spiked him to the Roman gibbet. Two thousand years ago, as he died, something miraculous happened. Like a sponge, he absorbed the sins of every one of us. Like a sponge, he took the sins of the world onto himself and made them his own. Two thousand years ago, Jesus died on the cross. He who knew no sin became sin. The good news is that all who believe in him and trust in him will not be punished for their sin because on the cross he was punished in our place.

Not only that, God forgot our sins. Our sins were blotted out, says the Scripture, buried in the deepest sea, remembered no more. I don't know about you, but I would hate to go to heaven if God remembered.

Can't you just see John Kyle, standing before the judgment seat and the Lord saying, "Kyle, we've been waiting for you." I don't know if they have a Kyle book, but if they open it up, I've got good news: There won't be any of the rotten, dirty things that he's done written in the Kyle book. It is forgotten.

There's one thing more. Besides taking our sin on himself and forgetting we ever sinned in the first place, he also "imputeth unto us his righteousness." That's out of the King James. I am an old King James man, and unfortunately many new versions don't have good words like *imputeth*. It's a great word. It means he gives us the credit for all the good things that he ever did.

I can't wait to get to glory. When they open my book, they're going to have under the name Tony Campolo all the good stuff that Jesus ever did. I'm going to be credited for it. It's going to be imputed unto me.

I wish my wife no harm, but I want her there when I arrive because I know when they start reading all the good stuff that Jesus ever did, she's going to say, "You didn't do all of that."

I'm going to say, "It's *his* book." I can say joyfully, "There is therefore now no condemnation for those who are in Christ Jesus" (Rom 8:1 RSV).

Perhaps you're thinking, "That's an interesting theological perspective. But there are varying views on salvation. There are Buddhist views and Confucian views and Marxist views. How can you be so narrow-minded to say that your view, the biblical view, the Christian view, is the only view?"

I was on an airplane coming from California to Philadelphia. I sat down next to this guy. It was the red-eye special, one o'clock in the morning, and he wanted to talk. He said, "What's your name?"

I said, "Tony Campolo."

He said, "What do you do?"

When I don't want to talk I say, "I'm a sociologist." And they say, "Oh, that's interesting." But if I really want to shut them up, I say, "Oh, I'm a Baptist evangelist." Generally that wipes the guy out right on the spot. So not wanting to talk at all, I said, "I'm a Baptist evangelist."

He said, "Do you know what I believe? *[I could hardly wait.]* I believe that going to heaven is like going to Philadelphia. There are many ways to Philadelphia. Some go by airplane. Some go by train. Some go by bus. Some drive by automobile. It doesn't make any difference how we go there. We all end up in the same place."

I said, "Profound," and went to sleep.

As we were coming into Philadelphia, the place was fogged in. The wind was blowing, the rain was beating on the plane, the wings were shaking, and it looked like the whole plane was going to come apart.

Everyone was nervous and tight. As we're circling in the fog, I said to the theological expert on my right, "I'm certainly glad the pilot doesn't agree with your theology."

"What do you mean?"

I said, "The people in the control booth are giving instructions to the pilot, 'Coming north by northwest, three degrees, you're on beam, you're on beam, don't deviate from beam.' I'm glad the pilot's not saying, 'There are many ways into the airport. There are many approaches we can take. There are many ways we can land this plane.' I'm glad he is saying, 'There's only one way we can land this plane, and I'm going to stay with it.' "

There is no other name whereby we be saved except the name of Jesus. This Jesus who died two thousand years ago on the cross, this Savior who is the only way to deliver us from sin, is a resurrected Jesus. And he comes to us even today. He is alive, and he is personally present in this room tonight. He is here. And a lot of people here need to accept him, and a lot of people here need to surrender to him.

The Cultural Jesus
But often people are turned off to Jesus because they don't really know what he's like. In the first chapter of Romans it says, "For since the creation of the world God's invisible qualities—his eternal power and divine nature—have been clearly seen, being understood from what has been made, so that men are without excuse. For although they knew God, they neither glorified him as God nor gave thanks to him, but their thinking became futile and their foolish hearts were darkened. Although they claimed to be wise, they became fools and exchanged the glory of the immortal God for images made to look like mortal man and birds and animals and reptiles. Therefore God gave them over in the sinful desires of their hearts to sexual impurity for the degrading of their bodies with one another. They exchanged the truth of God for a lie, and worshiped and served created things rather than the Creator" (Rom 1:20-25).

That is not a description of some preliterate society. That is a description of American society. Ours is a society that has taken Jesus and has recreated him in our own image. When I hear Jesus being proclaimed from the television stations across our country, from pulpits hither and yon, he comes across not as the biblical Jesus, not as the Jesus described in this book, but he comes across as a White, Anglo-Saxon, Protestant Republican. A Jesus who incarnates what we are, rather than a Jesus that incarnates the God of eternity, is not the Jesus who can save.

When I was teaching at the University of Pennsylvania, students would say, "I don't believe in God."

I would always say to them, "Describe to me this Jesus that you don't believe in. Describe to me this God you don't believe in." They usually thought that was a stupid question. But I would force them to answer it. And when they finished telling me what God was like, I would always congratulate them and say, "You're halfway to becoming a Christian because the greatest barrier to confronting and loving the real Jesus is being confused by the cultural description of Jesus that has emerged in our society."

We have in fact done something terrible. God created us in his image, but we have decided to return the favor, and we have created a God who is in our image.

You have a decision to make. Which God, which Jesus, do you choose to follow? Do you choose to follow the Jesus described in the Bible, the Jesus who died on the cross for your sins, the Jesus who was resurrected and is here tonight? Or do you choose to look at another Jesus, a Jesus that is created by the culture and that embodies and reflects our values?

What Car Would Jesus Buy?

What is the difference between the two? The differences are pronounced. The Jesus of the Bible differs from the Jesus of Scripture in what he asks of you. The biblical Jesus bids you come and give everything that you are, everything that you have to him. The biblical Jesus says, quite simply, "Read my book. Read my Scripture. Come learn of me. And then in your everyday life, be like me." Let this mind be in you which is also in Christ Jesus. To be a follower of the biblical Jesus is to do exactly what the biblical Jesus would do if the biblical Jesus were in your shoes and in your circumstances.

Nothing is more controversial than to be a follower and a disciple of Jesus Christ. Nothing is more dangerous than to live out the will of Jesus in today's contemporary world. First, it will change your whole monetary lifestyle. What you do with your money will change.

People ask me, "What do you mean? Are you suggesting that if I follow Jesus I won't be able to go out and buy a BMW?" *You got it!*

I know a lot of people who own BMWs. When they really get godly, they will repent of their BMWs because BMWs are luxury cars that symbolize conspicuous consumption instead of compassionate concern for the sufferings of the world.

Supposing that Jesus had to buy a car since there aren't donkeys on the highways anymore. If he had $40,000 and knew about the kids who are suffering and dying in Haiti, what kind of car would he buy? This is not irrelevant. This is where Christianity needs to be applied.

You've got to buy what Jesus would buy. You've got to dress with the kind of clothes that Jesus would dress in. There's no room for conspicuous consumption. This culture has in fact conditioned you to want more and more stuff you don't need so that while you are consumers of God's wealth, the hungry of the world suffer and the hungry of the world die.

It's time to repent of our affluence. Christians have lost the heart of the poor. Dr. Hestenes, my boss, said last night, "You're not a Christian in the full sense of the word until your heart is broken by the things that break the heart of Jesus."

At the college where I teach I urge all of our sociology majors to go to the Dominican Republic or Haiti on study tours during the month of January. I want them there. The first time I took a group of students there we stayed in a filthy, dirty home in a slum.

In the early morning the priest of the village invited us to walk with him. There was a flu epidemic. I had never seen anything like it. In the United States and Canada when people get the flu, they miss school. But when people are extremely malnourished and they get the flu, they die. As we wandered through the mud paths of the slum, mothers came out of their shacks that morning carrying the corpses of the children who had died during the night.

We went to the edge of the town, and we dug a ditch. And into the ditch we dropped these dead kids. We looked across the ditch as the priest prayed his prayer and the women screamed as only they can scream in the Dominican Republic.

I saw one of my students who was a basketball player. He was always macho. But he didn't look macho that day. Tears were streaming down his cheeks. His fists were clenched. His chin was trembling. And I knew, I knew that his heart had been broken by the things that broke the heart of Jesus. Blessed are they that mourn.

Tony, are you suggesting that you can't be rich and be a Christian at the same time? I'm not the guy that dreamed up the line that it's harder for rich people to enter the kingdom of heaven than for a camel to go through the eye of a needle. That was somebody else.

Tony, you're going to insult rich people. Do you have this world's goods? And can you see somebody with a desperate need and hold on to what you have while they suffer and die? If that's the case, 1 John 3:17–18 asks, "How then can you say you have the love of God in your heart?" That's what I'm asking.

If this offends you, be offended. Reject Jesus if you must, but you dare not take the biblical Jesus and turn him into something that he is not. He is the Jesus that confronts you and asks, "Are you willing to lay it on the line?" For unless a man, unless a woman, deny himself he cannot enter the kingdom of heaven.

I worry about a church that has forgotten what the Bible teaches. We evangelicals work overtime proving that the Bible is inerrant, and after we do, then we refuse to accept what it says. It not only says we have to have a new attitude toward wealth, it means we have to be radical in all kinds of ways.

The Dangerous Jesus
When I became a Christian, the Korean War was in progress. It was an incredible experience because I didn't know whether or not to accept the draft. I had a conversation with a colonel, and we argued back and forth.

He said to me, "What's your problem?"

"My problem is I want to do what Jesus would do."

"Could you get in a plane, fly over an enemy village and drop bombs?"

I said, "I could get in the plane. I could fly over the enemy village. But when I was about to release the bomb, at that moment I would have to say, 'Jesus, if you were in my place, would you drop the bombs?' "

And I remember the colonel yelling back to me, "That's the dumbest thing I've ever heard. Everybody knows Jesus wouldn't drop bombs!" That colonel probably knew more about Jesus than most Baptist preachers that I know.

Tony, this is getting upsetting. What you are talking about now is getting politically dangerous. But when did Christianity cease being politically dangerous? We are looking for a new breed of Christians who will come to the Sermon on the Mount and live it out with a radical commitment. The world urgently needs people radically committed to the biblical Jesus.

The cultural Jesus will create a church very different from the biblical Jesus. The church that is generated by the cultural deity that we have dreamed up out of our Protestant imagination is a honorary chairperson of a static institution. The biblical Jesus is the leader of a revolutionary movement that is destined to challenge this world and transform it into the kind of world that God willed for it to be.

If you get involved with this Jesus, you are going to become a dangerous person. If they send you to South Africa, you will not be able to tolerate the injustice of oppression that exists in that place. You will raise questions when our armies march off to war in places like Nicaragua. You will become a person who becomes dangerous because this church is committed to justice.

I am looking for a church that sends people into every avenue of life—into business, into the arts, into the educational sector, into the entertainment world—to be the revolutionary leaven that transforms the world. The task of the church is not to get ready for heaven. It's to communicate the kingdom of heaven in the midst of this world. The kingdom of this world will become the kingdom of our God.

When I read the life of John Wesley and hear about the great Wesleyan revivals (which incidently were initiated by students), I realize that Christianity can be an instrument for nonviolent change in a world that needs to be changed. When I read the stories of Charles Finney, the great revivalist of the 1800s, I realize that Jesus can be an infusing presence that transforms the world today as he did back then. The anti-slavery movement, the abolitionist movement, the feminist movement were all born out of the revivals of Charles Finney.

This is a historic moment because God wants to raise up a generation of men and women who will enter into every sector of society as agents of change, transforming the world into the kind of world he wills for it to be.

Is it always nonviolent? Yes, I believe it is. I believe we must stand up for truth and speak the prophetic word of God.

That's what I loved about Martin Luther King. He came marching out of Selma, and he meets that old Bull Connors. And there they are. Bull Connors has his guns. Bull Connors has his clubs. Bull Connors has his troops. And King and his followers got down on their knees and prayed. There is nothing more vulnerable than a person on his knees in prayer. And at the count of ten, Connors and his troops marched in, and they bashed in the heads of King's followers, and I saw them battered and beaten and plastered all over that road. I knew—as I saw that on live television—that God had just won, that the civil rights movement had just won.

I know you're thinking, "How do you figure it won? They got their heads bashed in. They got stomped. They got kicked. They got killed." You're right. But we Christians have a nasty habit of rising again.

The Love of Power

I want a church that changes the world not from a position of power but from a position of love and commitment. I get scared about Christians today because they are on power trips. We think that if we get enough power, if we get enough people in office, if we take over America, we can force America to be righteous. Why didn't Jesus ever think of that? I believe that we have to change the world with the weapons of the church and not the weapons of the world. We have another style, another way. It's loving servanthood. It's giving ourselves, it's moving in, it's caring, it's loving, it's redeeming, not destroying.

I can understand power because everybody loves power. I love power. One day when I was coming home from the University of Pennsylvania where I used to teach, I came down the expressway, and just as I crossed Cityline Avenue, I heard this kerplunk, kerplunk. A flat tire. So I pulled over and jacked up the car.

As I was changing the tire, I was listening to the radio which started to broadcast from the traffic helicopter. "Well, ladies and gentlemen, they're not going to get home tonight. They're backed up on the expressway all the way to Montgomery Avenue. They're standing still both directions on Cityline. The city of Phildelphia is a virtual standstill."

I wondered to myself, "What has brought the city of Philadelphia to a standstill? What has frozen the fair city of brotherly love? Why has Frank Rizzo's town suddenly been paralyzed?"

Then the announcer said, "There is a brown car just west of Cityline Avenue." That's me! That's my car! Little Tony Campolo has got the city of Philadelphia standing still! Mothers can't get home. Children are crying for their fathers. Business deals are falling through. Lovers are not meeting, and I am making it happen!

Who of us is immune to the lure of power? Who cannot be seduced by it? But the biblical Jesus is not into power. The biblical Jesus gave up power. He could have forced the world to be righteous, could he not? Instead he came and infuses people with his Spirit and calls on them to live sacrificially in love in this world.

A Hidden People

If I've been a little controversial, let me get *very* controversial. I have a friend in Brooklyn who is a pastor. He has a church in a dying community. Whenever I want a good story, I always call him because he always has good stories, even though he doesn't know it. I steal all his material.

"What happened last Tuesday?" I asked.

"Oh, that was weird," he said. "I had a funeral."

You see, he's a guy who makes so little that he has to do funerals to make a few bucks to keep himself going. He said the local undertaker had called with a funeral and nobody wanted to take it because the guy had died of AIDS. So he took the funeral.

"What was that like?"

"When I got there, it was weird. There were about twenty-five or thirty homosexuals sitting there. They sat there frozen with their hands on their laps. Their eyes were riveted straight ahead. They looked neither to the right nor to the left. I read some Scripture. I said some prayers. When the funeral was over, we went out and got into automobiles and drove out to the cemetery.

"I stood there at the edge of the grave as the casket went into the hole. Once again I read some Scripture. Once again I said some prayers. And when I had said the benediction and turned to leave, I realized that none of these homosexual men had budged. I turned back and said, 'Is there anything else I can do?'

"And one of them said, 'Yes, there's something else you can do. I haven't been to church for years. Actually I was looking forward to the funeral because I always love to hear them read the Twenty-third Psalm. Pastor, would you read the Twenty-third Psalm?' So I read the Twenty-third Psalm.

"When I finished another man said, 'There's a passage in the book of Romans, and it says that nothing can separate us from the love of God. Do you know that passage?' And I read to those homosexual men, 'Nothing can separate you from the love of God. Neither height, nor depth, nor things present, nor things to come, nor principalities, nor powers, nothing—*nothing* can separate you from the love of God—nothing can separate you from the love of God.' And I stood there near the grave reading to these homosexual men passages of Scripture upon request for almost an hour."

When I heard that, I cried. I really cried because I knew these men were hungry for the Word of God but would never set foot inside a church because they believed that the church despised them. And they're right.

Am I approving of the homosexual lifestyle? Certainly not! All I'm saying is, When are we going to start loving the people that nobody else will love?

Somebody asked me, "If you were the pastor of a big inner city church, what would you do?" They asked me that at a press conference yesterday. I said quite simply, "I would ask the church to mortgage the building, take the money and build a hospice for AIDS victims because I think we need to say something to the homosexual community."

There are Spanish-speaking people, Black people, Italian people in the inner city. I'm here to tell you there are approximately nine to ten million homosexuals, and the church of Jesus Christ has forced them to become a hidden people. It's about time that, without approving of sin, we love people.

I'm looking for a whole new mission enterprise. I'm looking for Christians who will set up Christian hospices for AIDS victims, for young men and women who will become doctors and nurses to take care of these people that some of our more secular doctors and nurses won't touch. It's time for Christians to create a daring church—a church that dares to love.

To Boldly Go Where No Man Has Gone Before
Lastly, the cultural Jesus only asks us to be reverent and to be religious. I am not calling you to be religious. I am calling you to take your life and say tonight, "Jesus, I love you. I love you so much, I want you to take my life, and I want you to use it to do something splendid. I want you to send me to those places where you need me to go. I'm here. Take me. If it's Africa, it's Africa. If it's Philadelphia, it's Philadelphia. If it's Buenos Aires, it's Buenos Aires. If it's Calcutta, it's Calcutta. I'll go where you want me to go, dear Lord. I'm yours."

The biblical Jesus wants to employ you in the place where he can use you to the optimum level. Why is that overseas? Because America is overstaffed. We have so many people coming out of colleges and universities these days that the society can't absorb them all. You don't have to go to work for General Motors. It'll survive without you. You don't even have to be a doctor in the United States, they've got enough. You certainly don't have to add to the supply of American lawyers.

What I love about "Star Trek" was the starship Enterprise skipping out into the darkness, and the voice saying, "Challenged to boldly go where no man has gone before." I'm here to call you to go where no one's ever gone, to do what no one's ever done, to be what no one's ever been. Being a missionary is hard. But most of the alternatives are very dull. If you want to be a Yuppie, that's OK. It's just boring, that's all. What do they do? Work all week, come home, sit in the Jacuzzi and tell each other it's wonderful.

In the last scene of *Death of a Salesman* when they lower Willie Lowman into the grave, his wife says, "Bif, Bif, why did he do it? Why did he kill himself? Why did he commit suicide? Why did he do it, Bif?"

And Bif says, "Ah shucks, Mom. Ah shucks, he had all the wrong dreams. He had all the wrong dreams." If there's anything that can be said about this generation, it's that you've got all the wrong dreams.

If you want to be a schoolteacher, why be in a place where they don't really need you? Why not let God take you and place you where you are absolutely essential? If you want to be a doctor, why not go where you're desperately needed? Why would anyone want to be a doctor where half of your patients aren't even sick when you can go to the place where the life and death of hundreds of people will be hanging on you daily.

I'm with old Oswald Smith. I don't see why anybody should hear the gospel twice before everyone has had a chance to hear it once. Give your lives over to Jesus. The needs are so horrendous. If you think you can't do it, you're crazy.

I was asked to be a counselor in a junior-high Christian camp. Everybody ought to be a counselor in a junior-high camp just once. If any Roman Catholics are here, you're right, there is a purgatory. We tried everything to get through to these kids what the gospel was all about. But nothing worked. Junior-high kids' concept of a good time is picking on people. And in this particular case, at this particular camp, there was a little boy who was suffering from cerebral palsy, and they began to pick on him.

They picked on little Billy. Oh, they picked on him. As he walked with his uncoordinated body, they would line up and imitate his grotesque movements. I watched him one day as he asked in his slow drawn-out speech, "Which way is the craft shop?" And the boys, mimicking his speech and movements, answered, "It's over there, Billy." And they laughed at him. I was irate.

But my furor reached it's highest pitch on Thursday morning when it was Billy's cabin's turn to give devotions. They had appointed Billy to be the speaker. They wanted to get him up in front to make fun of him. And as he dragged his way to the rostrum, you could hear the giggles rolling over the crowd. And it took little Billy almost five minutes to say, "Jesus . . . loves . . . me. . . . And . . . I . . . love . . . Jesus." When he finished, there was dead silence. I looked over my shoulder, and there were junior-high boys bawling all over the place. A revival broke out.

As I travel all over the world, I find missionaries and preachers everywhere I go who say, "Remember me, I was converted at that junior-high camp." We had tried everything. We even imported base-ball players whose batting averages had gone up since they had started praying. But in the end God chose not to use the superstars. He chose a kid with cerebral palsy to break the spirits of the haughty. He's that kind of God.

Give your life to Jesus no matter what you're like and no matter what you can do or can't do. He wants to take you. He wants to fill you with himself. And he wants to use you to do the work of the kingdom.

Tony Campolo, author, lecturer and evangelist, is chairman of the department of sociology and youth ministries at Eastern College.

15
Evangelism: The Heart of Missions

Becky Pippert

ONE OF THE THINGS THAT MOST AMUSES ME AS I TRAVEL IS HOW PEOPLE RE-
spond when I tell them what I do for a living. I was flying from New
York to California, and I sat down next to this guy who was a quintessential Southern-California type—gold chain, open collar, everything but the feathers, and very mellow. As we were talking, all of a
sudden he said, "Hey, what do you do for a living?"

And I said, "I'm in Christian work."

And he said, "Hey, that's cool. I wouldn't hold it against you."

And I said, "How thoughtful, I appreciate that."

A little later I was flying back from California to New York, and I
was sitting next to a quintessential New Yorker—tense. I was hanging
on by my fingertips in this conversation, and he said, "What do you
do for a living?"

And I said, "I'm in Christian work."

He said, "That's impossible."

I asked him why he was so shocked. He responded, "You look
normal!"

Soon after I was flying into Lubbock, Texas. I was in this little commuter plane, sitting next to a woman from Lubbock. Of the six people on the plane, five of them were obviously East Coast types with their *Wall Street Journals* and their briefcases and all. Then this woman from Lubbock asked me, "What do you do for a living?"

And I said, "I'm in Christian work." And she said, "Oh, honey, that's sweet. That's the sweetest thing. You sit right here now." Then she turned to all of the New Yorkers reading their *Wall Street Journals* and said, "This little girl over here works for Jesus."

Everybody put down their *Wall Street Journals* and looked over at me. And I said, "Ha, ha, ha, well, what can I say? It's a living, you know what I mean?"

However, I wonder if you hear what I am hearing. As I listen to questions, as I meet people, I try to hear the question behind the question. The question I so often hear is "What difference does it make to believe in God? Does it really make a difference?"

Does It Make a Difference?
While my husband had a fellowship at Harvard, one of the faculty members whom I had gotten to know came up to me an said, "Becky, I want to tell you something. I admire your faith, I really do. But I want to ask you a question. Do you really think it makes a difference to believe in God? Isn't life pretty much the same for all of us? Don't all of us really want to be loved? We all want to be a part of something. We don't want to be left out whether we believe in God or not. Isn't life difficult for all of us? I don't think cancer cells ask before entering a body, 'Excuse me, are you a praying man?' "

He continued, "Don't we all try to raise our children to do right and yet some go wrong and leave us brokenhearted? Don't most of us have conflict between morality and desire? Isn't life pretty much the same? Don't you fail morally as we do? Maybe Christians do better in some areas than others, but what about pride and hypocrisy and racism? Does it really make a difference?"

Does it?
There's been a lot of discussion these days about our need for mentors. The idea is that we need to see qualities that we admire demonstrated through people we see. Who are the mentors for the graduating class of 1987? In business it was Ivan Boesky, in politics it was Gary Hart, and in religion it was Jim Bakker. Now that's pretty sober-

ing. Even more sobering is that two of these three men came from strong evangelical roots. Two of these three men, at some point in their life, proclaimed a deep faith in God. We have to ask ourselves, "Does it make a difference to believe in God?"

Furthermore, I meet many Christians who are secretly discouraged. I doubt that there's a Christian in this auditorium that doesn't long for the grace to simply live what they believe. We begin our walk with God with great enthusiasm, and then slowly we begin to see that we may not love him as much as we thought we did. We understand obedience better, but we feel less inclined to pay the price. And we begin to say, "Do my problems and temptations make a mockery of faith? Does it make a difference to believe in God?"

And even the world is aware that we've got a problem. *Time* magazine did an entire issue on ethics. They entitled it, "Whatever Happened to Ethics? Assaulted by Sleaze, Scandal and Hypocrisy, America Searches for Its Moral Bearings."

Secular prophets are rising up and saying the kinds of things Christians should be saying. Garry Trudeau, who writes the cartoon strip *Doonesbury,* said in a commencement address, "We live in an age where men and women would rather be envied than esteemed. And when that happens, God help us." Dan Rather did a radio spot entitled, "Whatever Happened to Sin?" Ellen Goodman, the Boston Globe journalist, did a column on the goodness of guilt. Meg Greenfield of *Newsweek* did an article on the possibility of moral absolutes. Even the secular press corp, the group everybody loves to hate, has entitled this presidential campaign, "The Campaign of Character." And perhaps the most powerful of the secular prophets was Ted Koppel in his address at Duke for his commencement. And he said,

We have actually convinced ourselves that slogans will save us. Shoot up if you must, but use a clean needle. Enjoy sex whenever and with whomever you wish; but wear a condom.

No. The answer is no. Not no because it isn't cool or smart or because you might end up in jail or dying in an AIDS ward—but no because it's wrong. Because we have spent 5,000 years as a race of rational human beings trying to drag ourselves out of the primeval slime by searching for truth and moral absolutes. . . . In its purest form Truth is not a polite tap on the shoulder; it is a howling reproach. What Moses brought down from Mt. Sinai were not the Ten Suggestions. They are commandments.

What I am hearing from the secular prophets is "Where are you?

Wake up out there! What kind of contribution are you going to make?" Now I must say that when Christians try to make a contribution, often we are immediately lectured on the separation of church and state and told to go back to the pews. We need to make a contribution that is intelligent, sensitive and not self-righteous. But the question has to be asked, "If these secular prophets are saying this, does it make a difference?"

The Difference We Make

I want to say it does. It makes a tremendous difference believing in God. But we've gotten into trouble because we have forgotten what we already know. We have forgotten what the problem is and what the solution is. The problem according to the Scriptures is the human heart. It is the problem of sin. And the treatment for sin has always been grace. How did we come to forget? We live in strange times where we walk around acting as if we are basically wonderful people who occasionally do bad deeds. Even as early in our history as when the Constitution was written, they understood that human nature was treacherous and so designed a government to protect us from ourselves.

The problem hasn't changed. I think we've just developed short memories. What's the problem? The problem is sin. G. K. Chesterton said it as concisely as anyone I know when he was asked to respond to a magazine essay entitled, "What's Wrong with the Universe?" In what has to be the shortest essay in history, he wrote, "I am!"

The core of the problem is not psychological, emotional or spiritual. The core of the problem, rather, is spiritual. It is the problem of the heart. G. K. Chesterton said, "I find it amazing that modern people have rejected the doctrine of original sin when it's the only doctrine that can be empirically verified."

What's the solution? The solution is the grace of God that promises to change our heart of stone into a heart of flesh. Not overnight. To be converted doesn't make you a finished product. But God will help us with his grace to become new people.

The Crucifiers and the Crucified

How can we understand the problem and the solution? We need to look at the cross. The cross, if you're going to be a witness on your campus, will help you understand what the problem is and what the solution is. When you look at the cross, you really have to keep two images in mind. And the two images are these: we crucified him, and we were crucified with him. Both are true. We crucified him, and we were crucified with him.

Several years ago, after I had spoken at a conference, a lovely woman came and spoke to me. She was beautiful, she was godly, and she was tortured. She told me her story. She said that she and her fiancé, many years ago, had been the leaders of a youth group at her church. And they had a tremendous ministry. They were to get married in June and somewhere in that year they began to have sex. Then she discovered she was pregnant. She said she felt bad enough that the very thing that she was trying to counsel others not to do she was doing, but to find out that she was pregnant was much worse. She said that she knew the church could never handle her failure. (That is a tragic statement. A hospital can't handle the patients?) And so she said they decided to have an abortion.

"My wedding day," she went on, "was the worst day of my life. Becky, I love my husband. We've had many children, but I am tortured. I do not know where to go with my guilt because I believe I have murdered an innocent life. I am haunted by the question, What have I destroyed? I know that God loves and forgives but I cannot be released from this thought, How could I have ever murdered an innocent life?"

A thought came to me, but I was afraid to say it because she was so distraught, and I realized that if this thought wasn't from God, I could destroy her. But she kept saying, "How could I have done this? How could I have murdered an innocent life?"

I took a deep breath and said, "I don't know why you're so surprised. Because this isn't your first murder; it's your second."

Then I continued, "My dear friend, all of us are crucifiers when we look at the cross. You seem to feel more guilt over killing your own child than killing God's child. All of us, religious or irreligious, good or bad, aborters or nonaborters, all of us show up as crucifiers when we look at Jesus. Jesus died for all of our sin, past, present and future. Luther says we carry his very nails in our pockets. This isn't your first murder of an innocent. It's your second. And I'm just surprised that you're so surprised that you could do it."

She looked at me in amazement and stopped crying. And she said, "You're right; it's true. I have done something even worse than killing my own child. It doesn't matter that Jesus died 2,000 years ago; he died for all of our sins. And I have never felt the same remorse over killing God's son as in killing my son. But, Becky, what you're really telling me is that I've done something even worse than the worst thing that I could ever imagine." I nodded. "Becky, if the cross shows me as even worse than I thought, the cross also shows me that my evil has been absorbed and forgiven. Oh, Becky, talk about amazing grace." And I saw a woman literally transformed by a proper understanding of the cross.

You see she walked into the paradox of the cross. It's a cross that insists on highlighting our badness in order to leave us absolutely no doubt that whatever we have done has been forgiven. I come with remorse and guilt over one thing, and the paradox of the cross says, "You think you're bad? You're even worse off than you thought." And if the worst thing anyone could ever do, which is our sin that sent Jesus to the cross, if that's forgiven, how can what you are confessing not be forgiven as well?

The cross convinces us that we've been accepted at our worst. That is why we can face our problems without despair. That is why we can look at the darkest things in our lives without paralysis, because even the confession of sin can be seen in the context of hope and joy because God's solution is so wonderful.

There is no one who can ever say, "Well, God may love me, but if he really knew what I did . . ." God says, "I know what you've done. And you've done more than you even know you've done. And I love you, and I forgive you."

The second image we need to keep in mind as we consider the cross is that we were crucified with Christ.

Paul says, "I've got the most wonderful news. You're all dead!" And we say, "That guy was depressed on that day. I think he needed a Robert Schuller tape." But what does he mean? What does he mean that the cross enables us to die to something? What are we to die to? God wants us to be free from the things that destroy us. He wants us to be whole. And the cross tells us that we don't have to live under the domination of our compulsions and neuroses and sins any longer. We have been given a way out. We're not lost in enemy territory. We've come over into God's territory. We have been given a choice. And that choice is the life of the Spirit. And it is God's Spirit that will enable us, that will infuse us, that will help us to become the people that God longs for us to be. The battle of sin shall continue, I can assure you of that. But I hope you have tasted the Spirit of God and his life within you and his resources to make you new.

Evangelism and the Cross

Now what are the implications of the cross as we share our faith? I think one of the most wonderful implications of the cross is that it frees us from the pretense of innocence. We live in a world that is absolutely terrified of being discovered as being inadequate. For all of our bravado and boasting, the great secret about human beings is that we're so alike.

One of the wonderful things about the cross is that it frees us to own up to our badness and to not live in despair over it. To pretend to be innocent in light of the cross is, according to C. S. Lewis, like being a divorcée pretending to be a virgin. Integrity does not mean that we act as if we don't have a problem. Integrity means that we refuse to deny that we do have a problem. We must abandon our lust for innocence and any illusions we have about our innocence. No one can be innocent after the Fall. The sad truth is that we are all hopelessly centered on ourselves. We're self-absorbed, self-preoccupied, self-centered. There is no one's agenda that we care more about than our own. That's the disease of sin, and we've all got it.

The good news is that once we recognize we're not innocent, once we recognize we have a problem, Jesus says, "Help is on the way!" He wants to help us, and he wants to free us. The problem is that Christians seem to walk around acting as if it were a sin to admit that they were sinners.

I remember hearing a famous TV evangelist say, "People ask me, Do you struggle? Maybe I do, maybe I don't. I'm not going to tell you about it; I just go to God."

"Yeah, but don't you have tiffs with your wife or problems with your kids?"

He said, "Maybe I do, maybe I don't. I'm not going to tell you about it; I just go to God." Then he faced the camera and he said, "Oh, people, don't share all your problems and temptations. You just be a strong champion for Jesus. Be a man about it."

Why did that man have such difficulty even acknowledging that he was tempted? I am not suggesting that he share his sins before the television viewers, as interesting as that might be to hear. But I thought Paul said "I am the chief of sinners." Wouldn't that be refreshing over the TV airwaves? I remember when Paul said he had a thorn in his flesh. And I do not recall Jesus saying to Paul, "Oh, Paul, for crying out loud, would you just be quiet and be a man! Be a man, be a man! You know, buck up!" Jesus said, "I will not take this thorn in the flesh because I am glorified in your weakness."

Our TV evangelist did what we often do. He took a secular myth and spiritualized it. Really what he had done was to take the Lone Ranger motif and became a cowboy for Jesus. He was saying, "All I need is God and my horse. If I have a problem, I'll tell my horse." And they rode off into the sunset.

This is not biblical Christianity. What does the cross mean in how we evangelize? It means that we model repentance by acknowledging that we're not innocent. We have a problem, and God is helping us, and it is this process which makes us whole people.

The Democratic Cross

A second implication of the cross is that it is very democratic. Everybody is in trouble. We all share that. There isn't anybody who's better off than someone else. We all desperately need God. Consequently, there is no room for superiority, and there is no room for inferiority.

Now what does that mean then in context of evangelism? It means that we can't look at someone in the world and say, "Oh, I could never relate to them. They're not godly; they're sinners"—as if the experience of sin is something foreign to us.

During one of my husband Wes's assignments, we became very close to a couple who were political reporters. Helen was, by even the most secular standards, somewhat shocking. She was jazzy and wore very seductive clothes. I used to tease her that I couldn't imagine she had paid money for so little material. She smoked these slim cigars and always made a statement whenever she came into a room. I got to know her and found that she was bright and sensitive and tortured. Knowing that I knew she was married and had two children, she told me she, was having an affair with a man who was also married and had some children. And I loved her, and I shared my life with her. And I kept encouraging her to read the Bible.

I remember one day she came to my house and said, "Becky, I have a specific question about the Gospel of Mark."

And I said, "I knew it! I've been praying for you and loving you and always telling you that you need to read the Scriptures. It's because I've been doing that."

She said, "No, actually I was with my lover last week. He is Jewish, and very unexpectedly he turned to me and said, 'What do you think of Jesus?' "

And Helen said, "Pardon me?"

He explained, "Well, I'm a Jew. I know something of the Old Testament. I just decided I should know something of the New Testament, and I am so struck by Jesus. There is something very beautiful about who he is. So I thought you'd tell me."

She said, "Well, I'm very sorry, I take all my religious questions to Becky." So she had a list of all of her questions, and the parting word from her lover was, "Next week when we get together, among other things, I would like to study the Gospel of Mark!" Now, I have heard of unusual settings for a Bible study. This gets first place.

So I said, "Look, Helen, if you're really going to do a Bible study with him and you've never read the Bible, let's study it together." She said OK. So we began to read the Bible. The first time we were together, she got very nervous and uptight. And I said, "What's the matter?"

"Well, excuse me, but could I ask you a personal question?"

I said, "Yes."

She said, "Do you think the Bible would mind if I smoked a cigar?"

I said, "I think it can handle it, yeah."

So she lit up her cigar and we're into the passage, and she says, "Excuse me, but can I ask you another question?"

I said, "Sure."

And she said, "Do you think the Bible would mind if I had a glass of wine?"

I said, "You could always ask it, I don't know."

And so from that point on we met weekly to read the Scriptures, she with a glass of wine or a cigar in her hand. And we'd read about Jesus. It was amazing to see her responses.

And I remember one study in particular about when Jesus was with the prostitute at Simon's banquet. Helen looked at me and said, "Becky, all of my life I have thought that I was worth a piece of dirt. And I was sure that if there were a God, and I don't think there is, that he would concur with my analysis. Nobody needs to tell me I'm lost. I know I'm lost. I know I'm groping in the dark. I thought that if there is a God, he despises my blindness and my lostness.

"What I can't get over is that if you're lost, Jesus loves you more than ever. And if you're lost, and you know you're lost, you're probably close to the kingdom of God. Can you imagine that, me, close to the kingdom of God?"

And I said, "Oh, yes, I can."

And she said, "Becky, I can't get over Jesus."

I put down my Bible, and I began to cry, and I said, "You know, I've been a Christian for twenty years, and I can't get over Jesus either. I don't know what's going to happen to you. I hope with all my heart you become a Christian and that you find the wholeness that God wants. But you'll never be the same."

Helen broke off the relationship with that man. She is trying to make her marriage work. She and her husband were assigned overseas, and one day she called me. She said, "I haven't become a Christian yet, but I'm reading the Bible, and I'm reading the Bible to my children. I've found a minister and his wife. I don't know, Becky, they have an aroma that reminds me of you!" But she said, "Frankly, I find the church a little uptight."

I said, "Well, try wearing a few more clothes. Just a thought!"

I hope with all of my being that she comes to know God. But the question I want to ask you is, Why do I have the freedom to relate to a woman like this? Because the cross shows me that I'm no different. That is the wonder. Do you think it matters to Jesus that he went to the cross and died for one set of sins that happen to be different from another? The cross shows me I'm no different, and that's why we have this tremendous bond to the world. I need to be forgiven as desperately as Helen does. I can't put down a cup of coffee without needing someone to forgive me and love me, and that's the wonderful news—that we are loved and are forgiven. God does so much more for us than we could ever dream of doing for him. We must recognize that the cross leads us into relationships and into the world—out of joyful gratitude for all that God has done.

So what does it mean to go back to our campuses to be witnesses to the world? It means that we must refuse to feign innocence but strive for holiness. It means that we must reach out with open arms and embrace the world, embrace your roommate and your neighbor as deeply as God has embraced you. You do not need to go immediately overseas. Be a missionary on campus. Do the preparation, and love with the love of Jesus.

And lastly, the cross makes us witnesses to joy. That is the by-product of knowing Jesus. As G. K. Chesterton says, "Joy, which was the small publicity of the pagan, is the gigantic secret of the Christian."

Rebecca M. Pippert is an evangelist, speaker and author of the best-seller Out of the Saltshaker. *Portions of this address will appear in a forthcoming book and video series from Harper & Row Publishers.*

V
Reports
and
Testimonies

16
IFES
Urbana
Report

Chua Wee Hian

I WOULD LIKE TO INVITE YOU TO FLY WITH ME IN YOUR IMAGINATION ON A TEN-
minute trip around the world of IFES. Let's fasten our seat belts, but
first we must enter into a time machine and return to the year 1947.
There at Philip Brooks house, Harvard University, forty leaders representing ten national movements, including IVCF-USA and IVCF-Can-
ada, committed themselves to establishing an international fellowship which would seek to pool resources and share manpower so
that in every university of the world, there would be groups of Christians witnessing to our Lord Jesus.

Today there is evangelical student witness in over 130 nations.

Let's return to the present and fly to the vast continent of Africa.
Let's visit Nigeria. We have been invited to a prayer meeting. We
discover that Nigerian students often hold nightly prayer meetings.
What surprises us is that there are 300 or more people at this prayer
meeting, which may last for over two hours. When they pray, they
switch off all the lights, and if you are bold enough to open your eyes,
you will see flashing white teeth and also a tremendous volume of

prayers being offered to the Lord. Nigerian Christian students believe that God can do great things in answer to prayer and today in Nigeria, there are over 200 chapters with a membership of between 35,000–40,000 student members, making them the largest member movement in the IFES family today. These students unashamedly share their faith with their contemporaries and a good number are converted each year.

Last year in Ghana students at the University at Legon organized an evangelistic mission that went on for seven days. Each night over 1000 students would hear the claims of Christ clearly presented. On the docket one night was the theme of the Second Coming. All over the campus students had put up signs that indicate the Second Coming. One of the signs read: *Earthquakes!* And that night there was a severe earth tremor. The next night nearly the whole university turned up for the Bible reading, and over 300 people were converted.

Let's fly to Portuguese-speaking Africa, to Angola. This is a Marxist nation, caught up in the fray of civil war. We arrive at Luanda and are greeted by a Brazilian. In 1983 I was asked to send a staffworker to start Bible study groups in Angola. The person who made that request was himself converted when he was a medical student in Zaire. The man who led him to Christ was a Swiss IFES staffworker.

How do you find an instant worker, well versed in Portuguese and prepared to work in Angola? Because the Brazilian movement was an active member of the IFES family, we were able to present this challenge to them. They sent us one of their experienced workers whom God has used to build up several Bible study groups for students. Working closely under the Evangelical Alliance, this staffworker has even been asked to train national pastors. Like many IFES staff, she shares our concern to build up the church of Jesus Christ.

I'll never forget the story she told me about when she first met for prayer with an international group of supporters in Angola. Two words were repeated again and again: *Amen* and *hallelujah*. As I travel around the world, I hear these two words and a third again and again among Christians: the third is *Coca-Cola*. Now it is the clear intention of the Coca-Cola Company that every man and woman on planet earth should have at least one taste of Coke. Shouldn't we Christians have an even greater desire that every man and woman on our planet should hear at least once the claims of Jesus Christ?

Let's fly next to Latin America. We are greeted by warm "abrazos" from our Latin American brothers and sisters. We learn that it is not very easy for Christian students to meet together on the vast campuses because of limited time and the long period of time before someone actually graduates from university.

Let me take you to Peru. If we were to go to one of the universities in Lima, we would discover one of the strange ways our Peruvian brothers evangelize. There is tremendous competition to push one's ideology or faith. So you find students going up to a lecture hall and stopping the lecturer in the midst of his class. The lecturer usually protests. But being in the midst of a very democratic country, these Peruvian Christians say, "Let's have a vote. Let's see whether the majority of the class would want to hear about Jesus for two minutes." The vote takes place, and the majority, perhaps to get away from the boredom of the lecture, votes to hear a free presentation of the gospel. So these Peruvian students take two minutes to explain the claims of Jesus Christ and invite people afterwards to find out more about him.

Let's zoom in to Uruguay. Here in this secular state, we meet Daniel Salinas and Lucy Larrahondo from Colombia. Their movement, UCU, sent them as IFES workers. They labor alongside Judy Hanson of England and their brief was to win students for Christ and to build up an ongoing student movement. These are early days, but this team of young workers have learned to fast and pray and to concentrate on personal and small group evangelism. Today there are only a handful of students, but with your prayers, a strong national movement will emerge.

From Latin America we fly now to the Middle East. Here in predominantly Muslim countries, the going is tough. A colleague of mine had to say to a Muslim student, "If you really want to follow Jesus Christ, you may be signing your death warrant." This young man did, and within days was poisoned by his family.

But God has given a spirit of openness to Muslim students in North America and Europe. IFES has deployed various staffworkers to minister to these students and other international students.

Let me take you to Paris. At booktables you will find Iranian students and those from the Middle East asking searching questions about Jesus Christ. In a very quiet way and through evangelistic Bible studies, a few have come to faith in Christ.

We have three American couples—the Baileys in Austria, the Smiths in Germany and the Woolards in Belgium—mobilizing Christian students and families to befriend international students. In summers they are joined by large numbers of student team members, and through various coffee bars, evangelistic discussions, quite a number have committed their lives to Jesus Christ.

Let me now take you to Asia. Most of you know that it is almost impossible for missionaries to obtain visas to work in India. But through this seeming setback, God has been raising up Indian missionaries. At the last Urbana three years ago, I was speaking at a missionary conference organized by the Union of Evangelical Students of India. I was delighted to meet with Indian Bible translators, church planters and pioneer evangelists. This growing band of co-workers are going to the unreached peoples, especially in northern India. What was so gratifying is that a number of these missionaries received their missionary calls when they were students in our Indian movements.

I have also been very thankful to see the ways in which our students and graduates have penetrated various societies and nations. I think of my home country Singapore. The Foreign Minister—you would call him Secretary of State—was converted when he was a first-year student. He was thrown out of his family, and it was Christians who cared for him. Today he is an active elder in his local church. He serves as an ambassador both for his country and for the Lord himself.

A few weeks ago, many of us read of the tragic bombing at Eniskillen, Northern Ireland. Sixteen people were killed and eight of these men and women were from the local Presbyterian church. The world was surprised that families of those who lost their lives did not cry blood or the gallows for the IRA killers. Instead there was the message of forgiveness and reconciliation. So much so that a Catholic bishop was heard to have said, "We must learn to forgive like these Protestants." I discovered that the minister of this congregation is David Cupples. He was formerly the president of an Inter-Varsity chapter in Britain. How good it is to know that where there is crisis, we have former students making a clear stand for the gospel of reconciliation and forgiveness.

Finally, let's return from our swift journey back here to Urbana. What can you do to back up this work of God on the campuses and in the high schools of our world?

First, be our partners in prayer. I would like to urge you to subscribe regularly to the *PRAISE AND PRAYER* bulletin of IFES.

Second, be our partners in giving generously and sacrificially. We are embarking on pioneering projects in Mozambique, Haiti and Surinam, and we need to strengthen our work with international students. God has given us many opportunities for evangelism and training.

Third, be our partners also in serving. We need experienced staffworkers who could be loaned to assist on national movements in their training programs. Next year a staff couple from Singapore are planning to go to work in Zambia. We are always looking for young men and women with the gift of evangelism and friendship to serve on student teams in Spain, Italy and Belgium.

Come, my brothers and sisters! Let us work together for the glory of God!

Chua Wee Hian, a native of Singapore, is the general secretary of the International Fellowship of Evangelical Students (IFES) now based in London.

17
Testimonies: How I Heard God's Call

DURING THE CONVENTION SEVERAL PEOPLE TOLD HOW GOD CALLED THEM TO serve him abroad. Their testimonies are presented here in the order in which they spoke.

Dwight Nordstrom is a tentmaker, living in Beijing, China, and working as a General Electric Company divisional manager. Karen Purcell, a grade-school music teacher, spent two summers (1986 and 1987) with Overseas Training Camp Hong Kong/China and plans to return to China as a missionary. Kriengsak Chareonwongsak, a former professor of economics in his native Thailand, is pastor of the Hope of Bangkok Church, which together with its daughter churches has a combined membership of over 5000. Pat Devine, a veteran of InterVarsity Student Training in Missions program, is a Wycliffe Bible Translator, working in Togo in West Africa. Hey-Jin Kong, an MIT student who spent the summer of 1986 in Nigeria, plans to complete her medical degree with a view to future mission involvement. Eric Popp, a senior at Reformed Theological Seminary, has been accepted by Mission to the World to return to Japan as a church planter.

Dwight Nordstrom

The year was 1979. The place was Urbana, Illinois. The purpose: to attend the Urbana missionary conference to understand what God had for me. God used that conference to help me focus on my role in world evangelism, that is, on using my professional skills in law and business to serve as a tentmaker missionary among the Chinese.

But even before that conference, God had been working in my life preparing me for my present work. While growing up, I had many positive crosscultural experiences. For instance, I had the privilege of living for a while in a racially mixed neighborhood in Chicago, having relatives who were missionaries in Japan and also belonging to a mission-minded church. I went to Texas Christian University and studied religion and psychology. For graduate degrees, I went to Harvard Fletcher to study international law and also to the University of Houston and the Chinese University of Hong Kong.

While in graduate school and during the time in Houston, Texas, while I was helping my wife Mary to get her M.D., I was very active in ministry to international students. For instance, I have good memories of coordinating a van full of Chinese students going to Bear Trap Ranch in Colorado for Christmas. Another time, I invited about twenty to attend an American Thanksgiving. But have you ever tried to put a traditional American Thanksgiving meal on the table? Dry turkey is not that palatable to my Chinese friends, so I tried to give it a little Chinese flavor. I ended up with turkey and soy-sauce gravy.

In order to learn the Chinese language, which is essential if one desires to serve long-term in China, I played pro basketball in Taiwan. In the business world, I worked for Hughes Tool Company and for GE in their computer-aided design division. Both of these jobs have enabled me to work in mainland China. Presently, I live full time in Beijing and am manager for a division of GE. My professional skills have consistently put me in positions to be a witness for Jesus Christ, whether playing basketball in Taiwan as the only foreigner on the team, translating in a refugee camp in Hong Kong, working on an oil rig in southern Paraguay or taking forty-hour train rides across China. Having skills opened doors to share the gospel with the nationals who worked and traveled with me.

This conference will show you the great number of professional opportunities that exist throughout the world. Tonight, however, I'd like you to focus on the opportunities that exist in the Peoples Republic of China. But why China? I truly believe that China is the most exciting in terms of seeing results of any mission field in the world today. At no other time in the history of the world can it be said there are so many potentially successful opportunities to assist the national Christians in reaching one billion of their countrymen with the good news of Jesus the Christ.

Now, a note of caution. As we have seen, these one billion people are divided into many people groups, and you must focus on one. In the last nine years, China has made a strong statement of political will to become a modern, industrialized, fully participating member of the international community. Consequently, China needs foreign experts. Literally hundreds of Christians during these past nine years have gone to China to be professionals in teaching English and in teaching business and other subjects. Many others have gone as students studying Mandarin, oriental medicine and other areas. Unfortunately, not nearly as many Christians have come to China to be business or diplomatic personnel.

I want to offer a special challenge to you who are gifted in business. The opportunities to work in China are numerous. By 1990 bilateral trade between China and the U.S. should exceed 10 billion dollars. If you use a conservative ratio of sales per employee of one million dollars per employee, that means over 10,000 Americans will be needed to work in China.

Second, not only does the opportunity exist, but the tentmaker can be helpful. In my limited human wisdom, the two greatest needs I see for continued future church growth in China are an increase in the number and quality of biblically trained Chinese preachers, teachers and disciplers, and a decrease in the number and intensity of government or party sponsored acts of discrimination or persecution. I personally know of several business people who in many creative ways, within a system that does limit you, are assisting in meeting the needs of Christian teachers and are furthering an increase in religious tolerance both by working in the legal system and through personal relationships.

Eight years ago I was sitting in your seat on the threshold of my professional future. I accepted and will continue to accept the challenge of world evangelization in our generation by concentrating my efforts upon China. What is your decision?

Karen Purcell
"Does God speak Chinese?"

"Well, that's a silly question! Of course, he does! He is above all language, all culture, all differences. Everyone knows that!"

But while walking with me on a warm July night in Xian, China, my partner, Liu, asked that question with all seriousness of heart.

I would like to relate to you how God drew me into the heart of China and into the hearts of the dear people who call it home. My hope is that through this testimony China's faceless billion will gain a face for you, as I eventually focus on two very special people.

My heart races with excitement as I now have the hindsight to see God's marvelous sovereignty in bringing me to this place. If you would have told me before I started college that I would end up devoting my life in ministry to the Chinese, I would have laughed. I was going to be a high-school choral director. It is thrilling to see how God worked, not through a lightning-bolt missionary call, but a slow molding of my heart to match his heart for China. Here is how he brought my life from a blur of indecision into a clear focus, narrowed on the people of China.

It was September 1982, and it all started with Charlotte, my dorm neighbor. Week after week, she would stop by to invite me to the InterVarsity large group meeting or to the dorm prayer meetings. Week after week, I would say I was not interested. Her persistence soon paid off, and I attended my first prayer meeting. This trend continued. And the more meetings I attended, the more I was amazed. These people had a personal relationship with God. They spoke to him not with lofty words but with sincere pleas. The love of God displayed in these InterVarsity friends soon drew me to commit my life to Christ. My focus was narrowed—my life now belonged to God.

In June 1984 I was sitting on a beach towel on Illinois State University's quad, eating my lunch, and I realized at that moment that I should serve overseas—no stirring Billy Graham crusade, no uplifting Urbana conference or challenging InterVarsity event—just God and me and a bologna sandwich. A pastor had once told me that knowing God's will was 99% sanctified common sense, and through InterVarsity my eyes had been opened to the needs of a world dying without Christ. As I sat on that beach towel, I knew that there were millions of people stumbling apart from the light of Jesus, and I had that light. So why stay in a land where the gospel was already preached?

It made perfect sense. I knew I needed to go. Then the more I learned about missions, the more my heart ached for unreached people groups—among them Muslims, Hindus and Chinese peoples. I could not imagine that there were millions who had no opportunity to respond to Christ's love. Again, my focus was narrowed—my Lord wanted me overseas among the unreached.

In December of that same year, I was looking for a new roommate. Living in International House, I had always wanted an international roommate. God in his sovereignty provided Susie for me. Susie was a Chinese student from Malaysia who was soon to become a sister in Christ. Through Susie I came to develop some precious friendships with Chinese students at ISU. Isabella, Soo–Hua, Sim and Susie drew me into a deep appreciation of the Chinese culture. God used them to show me that American culture was not all it was cracked up to be. I was drawn to incorporate some of their cultural values into my own values and to drop my subtle feelings of American superiority. Again, my focus was narrowed—I wanted to serve the Chinese people.

In January 1986 I attended Mandate 86, the first Midwest missions conference for college students. It was there that I stumbled on the brochure for InterVarsity's Overseas Training Camp for Hong Kong and China. I had spoken often of my love for God, the Chinese people and my desire to go overseas. Now, here in my hand, was the perfect opportunity to put feet to my words. The typical obstacles to going overseas came into my path, and God faithfully removed them all. There were my parents: "Karen, you can't go—you'll contract some disease! Where will you get that kind of money? Why don't you become a famous Christian singer? You could reach more people that way. How could you leave the family?"

Praise the Lord! God changes hearts! My parents are now my most faithful supporters as they have let go and let God lead me wherever he chooses. After going overseas for two summers with OTC–Hong Kong/China, I grew to deeply love the people of China. Again, my focus was narrowed—the Lord wanted me in China.

On our OTC China trips, we had the awesome privilege of being involved in cultural exchange camps with university students in Xian (1986) and Beijing (1987). We were not encouraged to profess our faith openly unless they asked us about our belief in God. Many of the Chinese students inevitably did ask questions as they took notice of the depth and sincerity of love we had for one another and for them. But they were amazed that an intelligent college student would believe in God. To someone who has grown up with atheism, belief in God seems to be utter foolishness. Science and technology have become their god; economic progress, their savior.

We saw God do a marvelous work as they came to respect us as believers in God. Through these camps the Lord provided two very precious friends—Liu in Xian and Ronghui in Beijing. Again, my focus was narrowed—I was called to bring the love of God to my Chinese partners, Liu and Ronghui.

Liu was an unusually outgoing girl. We hit it off from the start and thoroughly enjoyed being together. Although we talked about everything under the sun, she did not ask a single question about my faith until that final warm July night. The conversation began as she said, "It is hard for me to understand how you trust God." She openly expressed that as a Communist Party member she could not believe in God. My heart aches because she does not even consider belief in God as an open option for herself.

Ronghui was a fun-loving yet extremely shy computer student. I was never able to share my faith with Ronghui, and I was tempted to leave feeling like a failure. So many others had spent hours talking about God—Tom sharing with Zhao, Bonnie with Sharon, Gary with Mao—but my lips remained silent. I left feeling as if Ronghui was left untouched by the love of Jesus.

Her letter which arrived two months later reduced me to tears. Ronghui had written, "This is my first letter written in English. Maybe there are many mistakes, but our friendship will not be influenced. It is two months since we said "Good-bye" at the middle school. Do you remember that time? Many cried except you and me. I think smiling is better than crying. Of course, I missed you, but I don't want to show it by tears. My English is not good enough to express my feelings." God *had* touched her heart. There *was* a person under that cool exterior. Even when I felt like a failure, our Lord was faithful to his promises.

Does God speak Chinese?

Having seen him do so in China, I can answer with a confident yes, but he yearns to speak it more. He longs to speak it to the billion inhabitants of China. He longs to speak it to China's university students. He longs to speak it to my friends, Liu and Ronghui. As couriers of his gospel, it is up to us to give him the chance.

Will you give him the chance?

Kriengsak Chareonwongsak

Brought up in a Buddhist family, I had never seen a Bible, a tract, a Christian or a Protestant church before I left for studies overseas at the age of 16. While I was a student in Thailand, I spent much time reading books on religion, philosophy and politics to find the meaning of life. During that time I devoted all my weekends to charitable activities such as community development projects in remote villages of Thailand, translating books into Braille for the blind, visiting slums and orphanages, helping the poor—all with the expectation of decreasing the vast gap between the rich and poor and changing social values.

Spending time doing all these things did not add any satisfaction to my life, and nothing really changed. At that critical time, as I was groping around and toying with Marxist idealism, my grades in school opened the opportunity for me to spend my senior year in high school as an exchange student in Wisconsin. After spending a year in the States, I returned home with the hope of attending a university in Bangkok where I could continue to explore the Marxist ideology of seeing a society of equality with people being helped.

My plans abruptly ended when the government offered me a scholarship to study in Australia, and my father pressured me into accepting it. Everybody who knew me saw that the road for a successful political career was well paved.

While studying at Monash University in Melbourne, Australia, a friend who always sat next to me during lecture hours befriended me. I noticed that he always had an old, worn-down book on his desk, and the words *HOLY BIBLE* were inscribed on it.

He witnessed to me about Jesus every day, and with Oriental politeness I listened with deaf ears. Each Sunday he would come over and knock at my door and invite me to go to church, and each time I would respond with a polite, "Not today, maybe next time."

Even though I didn't really care about what this friend said about God, his whole lifestyle impressed me. No matter how cold or rainy the weather was, he would go and help the more disadvantaged students and tutor them. I secretly admired this man, but I could not figure out why he was so committed to his faith. I knew he was a good person, but what a wimp! I was in search of the real meaning of life, and I was not going to waste time on this Jesus faith.

One day, as a professor was explaining about a mathematical formula, I noticed that he had made a mistake, so I pointed it out. The professor got rather upset, and we spent at least fifteen minutes discussing the problem. My Singaporean friend agreed that I was right. Later on the professor agreed as well, and I began to see that my friend was not so dumb after all. Being a Christian did not necessarily mean that one had a soft brain!

With a new attitude towards his intellectual capabilities, that evening I went straight to his room and asked him to tell me clearly everything about this Jesus. This time I was intent on listening because he might hold the very answer I had long been searching for.

The experience of my life took place then and there. God moved in my heart, and my whole thought pattern was overcome by the Holy Spirit. I realized how wrong I had been in attempting to do good deeds with the hope of seeing the truth revealed. While my friend was praying, my mind spun around and around and finally stilled with a sincere, "I want to invite Jesus into my life."

God revealed to me that Jesus was the truth. Right then and there, as I accepted Jesus Christ, I felt a refreshing peace and joy abounding in my heart. I was nineteen then.

A few days after that, as I returned from a birthday party of a Christian friend around midnight, exhausted and ready for bed, I stepped into my room and was startled by the tangible presence of God. The experience had a strong impact, and I could do nothing else but kneel down by my bed and pray. I just said, "Lord, I commit my whole life to you."

Immediately strange words stormed out of my mouth. I found out later that this was the gift of tongues. Nobody had taught or mentioned to me anything about this before, and the church that I went to believed that such gifts ended with the apostolic age. Besides, I had never heard anyone speak in tongues. Right then the sound of the wind blowing filled the room, but outside the window all the trees stood motionless.

Through that experience, God gave me a new understanding of the supernatural aspects of Christian faith. The Bible became alive within me, and I felt a definite empowerment of the Holy Spirit.

As I completed my bachelor's degree education, the university offered me a scholarship for advanced studies, so I stayed on, earning a Ph.D. in economics. During this time I met my wife, the only other Thai Christian there. She was working toward her master's degree. Our projected future was one of professional prominence and financial security.

However, God had other plans. Early one morning in 1976 God spoke clearly to me and told me to go back and plant churches in each of the 685 districts of Thailand by the year 2000. I was stunned because becoming a preacher or a pastor had never crossed my mind since my life was humanly destined for government services.

From that day I started watching God do wonderful things through and around me. He was training me from scratch, by on-the-job training, in evangelism, discipling, preaching, teaching and other ministries. His target group for me was the student body at the universities. I also developed myself through theological instruction and much personal study.

Five years after receiving this God-given vision, we returned home to Thailand, and I accepted a teaching position at the graduate school of economics at a university in Bangkok. My employment was teaching economics but my passion and dream was to fulfill the divine vision of planting churches.

We rented a hospital room for our first meeting in September 1981 with five members and a few onlookers. About six months later the room became too small, and the meeting was then moved to the hospital's chapel. Fourteen months later this too became overcrowded, and we took a step of faith, renting the Crystal Ballroom of the Sheraton Hotel. Attendance at that time was 250. Growth continued and the place became tight. In November 1984 we took another step of faith and took out a three-year lease on the Oscar Theatre. At the time attendance was only 300. Now in December 1987, our membership is 2773 at the Hope of Bangkok Church. We also have twenty daughter churches and preaching points in major cities of Thailand with a combined membership of about 5000 people. This has taken place all within the past six years.

Consider the fact that missionaries first entered Thailand in 1828 and in 1900, according to David B. Barrett's *World Christian Encyclopedia,* there were 90.8% Buddhists, 4.0% Chinese Folk Religionists and only .4% Christians in Thailand. By 1986 there were 92.1% Buddhists and 0.6% Christians. After 160 years of missionary toil, there has not been much increase in the number of Christians; however, the beginning of an exciting new day for church planting in Thailand has come. The growth of this indigenous church is the genuine work of God as the movement is bathed in prayer.

The church is broken down into cell groups of which there are 296 at present. These cell groups, consisting of 7-10 members each, are

the main life and thrust of the church as they stress personal discipleship and caring for each individual's spiritual, physical and emotional needs. By the year 2000, apart from planting a church in each
of the 685 districts, we also plan to establish 100,000 cell groups to
respond to the spiritual needs of the projected population of 10 million people in Bangkok alone.

To support such rapid growth, leadership training is vital. In association with the church, Thailand Bible Seminary was established to
offer four levels of training: Christian Life Course, School of Ministry,
Bachelor of Theology and Master of Divinity. All these courses com-
bine high-level academic teaching with practical in-service training
in discipleship while also providing the example and model of effec-
tive church growth and church planting. Leaders and potential leaders are trained to pioneer and pastor strong growing churches. Over
300 leaders have been through the course, and most of them are
either serving as leaders in daughter churches or have continued with
advanced training.

God has done miracles in this stunted Buddhist land, and I believe
he has greater plans in store for reviving the whole nation as he
raised more and more young people to join together in this great
reap. The Hope of Bangkok Church, which was started in 1981 by
Thai leadership, is now the largest and fastest-growing local church
in Thailand. Though we truly praise God for what he has done so far,
we are not prepared to stop since over 99% of the Thai's have yet
to receive the gospel of our Savior. God's grace is sufficient, and we
believe our race will be won.

Pat Devine
If you had asked me seven years ago if I ever thought I'd be a missionary, I would have laughed and said, "No way!" Seven years ago
I wasn't even a Christian. I was a freshman music major, and I had
my own plans for my life. I was going to be a classical percussionist
and play in a symphony orchestra. But God had other plans for my
life. He put in my path a freshman roommate who was a Christian.
She lived the Christian life before me and, by God's grace, halfway
through my sophomore year I gave my heart to the Lord Jesus.

At that time, I told the Lord that I was willing to do anything, be
anything or go anywhere that he wanted. Frankly, I had no idea what
I was in for when I prayed that prayer. Less than a month later I was
at a missions conference. In fact, it was an Urbana Onward Confer-

ence. That same roommate that had led me to the Lord had been at Urbana 81, and so I accompanied her to the follow-up conference.

There I began to hear about unreached peoples and the estimate that 2.7 billion people are beyond the reach of the gospel. So I began to ask myself, "I have the Good News of Jesus, but what am I doing with it?" Well, as I began to consider my involvement, I faced a really tough question: What does a classical percussionist do overseas in missions? It has been lightly suggested that I could "drum for Jesus," but that didn't seem likely. So how did I choose Bible translation?

More than anything else my choice of Bible translation was influenced by a cassette tape my friend brought home from Urbana 81. It was a talk given by Marilyn Laszlo. She's been a member with Wycliffe Bible Translators for a number of years working in Papua New Guinea. Her message was very powerful, and the Lord really used her to speak to me. For the first time I realized that the world has approximately 5,000 languages, 3,000 of which still do not have the Bible.

How many Bibles do you own or have access to? Do you realize that there are millions of people who not only don't own a Bible, but don't have access to even one word of Scripture in their own mother tongue? Imagine never being able to read God's Word for yourself. "Well," I said after hearing that tape, "maybe I could be a Bible translator."

The Lord has indeed graciously guided me and opened the doors before me. After becoming part of a rather missions-minded Inter-Varsity chapter, I learned of InterVarsity's STIM program (Student Training in Missions). Through it I received some excellent crosscultural training, and then I went overseas and had a marvelous time in the Philippines. I had the privilege of working with Wycliffe Bible Translators and came home saying, "I think I'd like working with those people." Sure enough, here I am! Now I'm a member with Wycliffe, and I've been assigned to work in a little country in West Africa called Togo. I'm excited about the opportunity I'll have of learning another language, reducing it to writing, teaching the people how to read and write their own language, and then giving them God's precious Word for the first time in their own language. What a privilege!

There's just one other thing I'd like to say, because I'm afraid of something. I'm afraid you're going to think I'm someone special—somehow unique or specially gifted—not like you. After all, you could never speak before all these people, right? The fact is that I am not anybody special. I feel very inadequate for the tasks that God is putting before me—including speaking before all of you. There have been many times in the last year when I have said to him, "Surely, Lord, you can find someone better able to do this work than me. It's not that I don't want the work done. I do. It's just that I don't know if I can do the job as well as I'd like to see it done." But as I raise these objections, do you know what his response seems to be? "Pat, I didn't call you to Bible translation because I needed you. And I didn't call you because you're particularly useful or worthy of the task. But I have called you that in my mysterious way I might glorify myself through your weakness."

What he desires from each of us is that we be willing to lay everything—our strengths *and* our weaknesses—on the altar before him and say, "Lord, whatever you want to do with me, I'm willing."

Hey-Jin Kong

When I first arrived on the MIT campus as a three-month-old Christian, I was happy to be invited by an InterVarsity student to be a part of his Bible study. Through that Bible study, along with a friend who took time each Saturday morning to study the Scripture with me and challenge me in my relationship with God, I began to see what it really takes to follow Christ. The summer of my freshman year, I worked as a volunteer staff at a Young Life summer camp, and each week I saw fifty to a hundred high-school students accepting Christ as their Savior. Such response led me to believe that God desires everyone in the world to hear his good news at least once.

Coming back to MIT as a sophomore, I heard of Student Training in Mission (STIM) once again. This time, however, I saw in the program a perfect chance to act on the vision for mission that God had given me during the summer. Thus I made my decision to go overseas the following summer on a short-term mission project. Through STIM training, I began to understand God's plan to redeem the world and our responsibility in carrying his message to people who have never heard.

I decided to go to Nigeria because I wanted to be placed in a culture unfamiliar to me so that I might learn to completely trust in God. But before I even reached Nigeria, God began to answer that prayer. Originally, I was set to go as a part of the OTC-Nigeria team. Two weeks prior to departure, I received a letter from the director of the program telling me that the trip had been cancelled. I still remember feeling confused and somewhat neglected as I sat with that letter in my hand. It seemed like God was backing out on me after all the effort I put into fund raising and persuading my parents that I should go.

Yet, within a couple of days, I was relocated in another InterVarsity project going to Nigeria. I did not know anything about the new project—nothing about who I would be working with, what kind of work we would be doing and where in Nigeria we were going. Upon arriving at orientation, I found out that we would be involved all summer in what we later called hut-to-hut evangelism. God must have a sense of humor. When I was originally planning my summer, I had said that I would go anywhere as long as I didn't have to do evangelism. Yet God was reaching me through these changes of plans. He was teaching me that I have to be obedient to him, not just in my decision to go, but in every aspect of carrying out that decision.

Once in Nigeria, I soon learned to enjoy evangelism. My first sharing experience was a nervous one, but I felt secure knowing that God was beside me and that my teammates were praying with me. As I shared with the people of Nigeria, the meaning of God's Word became alive for me and my excitement for knowing God grew. From time to time, the people from the village would come to the house where our team was staying and tell us of their decisions to follow Christ. That God would use our presence in the village in such a visible way was amazing to me, and seeing people come to Christ made even the difficult times worthwhile for us.

Then, too, living without resources we were used to—such as electricity, running water, privacy or food to our liking—I learned to rely on God for daily needs and to appreciate the abundant life we have in the States. I also learned to appreciate the simplicity of life that many people around the world lead.

Overall, I went into the summer thinking that it would be a once-in-a-lifetime experience, but came home seriously considering entering a long-term mission. I cannot understand how God changed my heart completely that summer. I know that he has shown me the value, the joy and the need of sharing his Word to people of other nations. I am very thankful for the way God used my summer to show me what a big God he really is. I have also gained Nigerian friends—people who were interpreters for us that summer and who still write and support me in prayer. One of them, named Reuben, is coming to the States to study at a Bible college, so that he might serve his congregation better when he returns. He is in financial need, and I have begun some fund raising for him. I am glad to be involved in Nigerian ministry in this way and also through prayer for the Nigerian student movement.

As I plan to go to medical school, I want to be aware of how God could use my plans overseas or in an urban setting. I have wanted to be a doctor as long as I can remember, and it is exciting to see how my plans are taking on a greater significance because of my relationship to Christ Jesus.

Even in Nigeria, there were times when I felt very inadequate to serve God. And I will never forget the encouragement of my team-mate Tom, who pointed out from 1 Corinthians that "Knowledge puffs up, but love builds up." No matter how knowledgeable we are in Scripture or in God's ways, it is only the deep love for Christ and people around us that will motivate us to serve God, no matter how minute our roles seem.

Eric Popp

This past week I've had the opportunity to speak to a number of students in the Huff Gym about possibilities available in missions. And a question has come up several times from students that are seeking to determine where God would have them in missions. And that question is, How did you get involved in missions? or, How did you know that God wanted you to go as a career missionary?

I became a Christian in junior-high school, and in high school I became very active in my church's youth group and in a campus ministry of my high-school campus. I came to realize that I had a responsibility to be involved in evangelism. At that time my sense of need to be telling others about Christ was mainly limited to those around me. Even though my home church was very mission-minded, and even though I had friends that had gone on summer missions projects, it never clicked in my head that I needed to be concerned about missions.

In my senior year of high school I went to a life-objectives confer-ence, and there I began to consider whether I should be involved in missions at some time. But it seemed like something five or ten years down the road. At that time in my life that was in the very distant future.

The fall of 1978 I entered the University of Tennessee at Chattanooga and began studying mechanical engineering. My home church was located right across the street from the school, and that same fall when they had their mission conference, I was able to attend many of the noon and evening meetings. The speaker there shared with me some things I had never heard before. He shared some specifics about the needs of the world. He explained that at that time 96% of Christian workers minister to 10% of the world—that portion of the world that speak English, leaving only 4% to minister to the rest of the world.

Being an engineer, those numbers and statistics had their effect on me, and my mind began to open up to the needs around the world. At that conference I made a commitment to go where God wanted me to go and to do what God wanted me to do. I didn't know at that time if that would mean overseas service or not. But I knew that if I was to learn where God wanted me, I needed to start investigating more about missions.

That spring I read a missionary biography concerning Jim Elliot, *Through Gates of Splendor,* and that book took my concern for missions from my head into my heart. I decided that that summer, after my freshman year at UCC, I would go on a summer mission project. I went to Surinam, South America, to work on a jungle air strip. While I was there, I was able to see a lot of the spiritual needs among the Indians there.

I came back to the States with a renewed enthusiasm about missions, thinking, "Well, I ought to quit school, pack my bags and head for the mission field." But I realized that that wasn't the best action to take. Instead I channeled my mission enthusiasm and my mission energy into three areas: a local ministry, missions education and missions involvement.

For my local ministry, I became active in the InterVarsity chapter at our college in a leadership position. As we sought to evangelize there, God blessed our ministry, bringing our large group from only seventeen members to seventy members. Also we had a number of small groups meeting throughout the week.

For mission education I began writing a missionary. During my years in school I attended two Urbanas. I also attended another InterVarsity conference called Haystack 81. Haystack 81 commemorated the 175th anniversary of a prayer meeting that led to the forming of the first North American mission society.

For my mission involvement, I got involved with six or seven others in a prayer group that grew out of Urbana. We met regularly each week to pray for different countries around the world. By the time I graduated I knew that all Christians needed to be involved in missions either as goers or as senders. From what I knew, I wanted to be one of those goers, but I still had a lot of questions on my mind. Could I survive in another culture for more than a few months? Did God want me to use my mechanical-engineering degree on the field, or did he want me to be involved in some other work on the field?

To find answers to these questions, I decided to apply to a two-year program—Missions to the World. They asked if I would go to Japan to work in an evangelism program as an English teacher. I said sure and I went. During that time God confirmed that he indeed wanted me as a career missionary. So I returned to the States with my missions interest more focused and entered seminary to prepare as a church planter to return to Japan. Just this past month I was approved to begin raising support as a missionary of church planning in Japan. It took ten years for God to bring me to this point, but he did. And he did it as I was faithful to respond to the mission opportunities that he had put before me.

I'd like to challenge you. As you consider where God would have you in world missions for the long haul, would you first consider where God would have you involved in missions right now? He will be faithful to show you what your part should be in proclaiming to the world the gospel of Jesus Christ.